American Lives / *Series editor:* Tobias Wolff

Works Cited: *An Alphabetical Odyssey of Mayhem and Misbehavior*

_To Bryce—

who is running
the ship.
Best —

BRANDON R. SCHRAND

University of Nebraska Press / Lincoln and London

Library of Congress Cataloging-in-Publication Data
Schrand, Brandon R.
Works cited : an alphabetical odyssey of mayhem and misbehavior / Brandon R. Schrand.
p. cm.
Includes bibliographical references.
ISBN 978-0-8032-4337-8 (pbk.: alk. paper) 1. Schrand, Brandon R.—Books and reading. 2. Influence (Literary, artistic, etc.). I. Title.
PS3619.C4618W67 2013
814'.6—dc23   2012037051

Set in ITC New Baskerville by Laura Wellington. Designed by A. Shahan.

For Kelli, the strongest person I know.

"In the days of my youth, I was told what it means to be a man."—LED ZEPPELIN, "Good Times, Bad Times"

"A book can be like the voice of God, telling us what to think of ourselves."—GEORGE SAUNDERS

Works Cited

Abbey, Edward. *Desert Solitaire: A Season in the Wilderness*. New York: Ballantine, 1971. 1

Brinley, Bertrand R. *The Mad Scientists' Club*. New York: Scholastic, 1965. 5

The Children's Bible. Racine WI: Golden Press, 1965. 8

Clemens, Samuel Langhorne. *The Adventures of Huckleberry Finn*. Racine WI: Golden Press, 1965. 12

Dickens, Charles. *Great Expectations*. New York: Bantam, 1982. 15

Emerson, Ralph Waldo. *Essays of Ralph Waldo Emerson*. Introduction by Carl Van Doren. New York: Literary Classics, 1945. 22

Fitzgerald, F. Scott. *The Great Gatsby*. New York: Macmillan, 1992. 34

Flaubert, Gustave. *Madame Bovary: Life in a Country Town*. Vol. 2 of *Norton Anthology of World Masterpieces*, 6th ed., edited by Maynard Mack, Bernard M. W. Knox, John C. McGalliard, P. M. Pasinetti, Howard E. Hugo, Patricia Meyer Spacks, Rene Wellek, Kenneth Douglas, and Sarah Lawall. New York: Norton, 1992. 49

Hacker, Diane. *The Bedford Handbook for Writers*. 3rd ed. Boston: Bedford Books of St. Martin's Press, 1991. 57

Hemingway, Ernest. *The Old Man and the Sea*. New York: Macmillan, 1980. 69

———. *The Sun Also Rises*. New York: Macmillan, 1987. 69

Hinton, S. E. *The Outsiders*. New York: Laurel Leaf, 1968. 83

Hornby, Nick. *High Fidelity*. New York: Riverhead, 1995. 87

Not Your Usual List of Acknowledgments

How does one come out on the other end intact? How does one survive the trappings of his own design? How does one, for instance, right such a foolish course that leads to—among other unseemly outcomes—jail (see pages 1, 52, 120 [a near miss], and 155), the wasteland of academic (college/high school) flunkydom (4, 26, 47, 69, etc.), the trough of too much drink (16, 22, 87, 88, 91, 97, 101, 119–22, 139–42, 151, etc.), the basement worlds of frat-boy sexual exploits and failed relationships (50, 51, 73–75, 89–95, 202–7, etc.), bar-crawling, deadbeat husbandom (100–110, 119–23, 155, etc)? And when he does finally emerge as a man and not a boy, as a husband and not a lover, as a father and not a son of misbehavior, what must he acknowledge for his implausible fortune?

A lot, as it turns out, and though I won't get into all of what needs acknowledging here, I will own up to the following:

I acknowledge, for instance, that I was too much boy for too long, too easily swayed by the books that I read. Books that say you can do anything you want, consequences be damned. Just follow the stories. Stories that say you can be anyone—and that it's fine, necessary even, to live out a fiction. Stories that say you can coast all your life on charm and apology. Stories that say you will live forever.

I acknowledge, too, that the boy within isn't entirely gone, that he swims up on a daily basis asking for one more martini, a cigarette, or to gaze a moment too long on a beautiful woman. But I also have to acknowledge that in the ongoing war of man vs. boy, the man wins. Usually. Or at the very least, the man has come to terms with the boy, his symbiote.

Finally, I acknowledge that books themselves cannot save your life. Not in any literal sense. But if I misread my ways into mayhem and misbehavior for so many years, I was able, finally, to read my way to some kind of safety. That journey is this story.

YOUR USUAL MEMOIR/NONFICTION DISCLAIMER: While this book is a work of nonfiction, the names and certain identifiable characteristics of people mentioned here have been changed. Some haven't been named at all, especially those who have been on the other side of the law.

Abbey, Edward. *Desert Solitaire: A Season in the Wilderness.* New York: Ballantine, 1971.

Sometimes I imagine the scene from above, as if camera-shot from a helicopter. The great wash of Arizona desert, that thread of leaden highway, blots of creosote and greasewood, an arroyo, and there, near the road, the flashing lights, blues and reds, the squad cars. Zoom in and you can see three young men, boys really, handcuffed. Zoom in closer to see their faces. The one in the middle, the thin one: that's me. It's April 1992 and I'm a nineteen-year-old kid who, along with his two fraternity brothers, have just been popped for a quarter-ounce of weed. It's not that big of a deal. It's not like we were these badass drug runners or anything. We were just three fraternity boys who wanted to go for a drive and smoke a little pot and listen to The Doors, and who happened to be speeding in the wrong place at the wrong time. We had fallen into a dragnet, a nine-car police roadblock, a random screen they throw down because, evidently, there is the occasional drug-thug who runs his junk up and down those ghosted desert roads. So our bust was small time. No big whoop. Unless, of course, you happen to be just inside the Arizona state line, as we were, and learn that possession of marijuana is a felony offense. Then it's kind of a big whoop.

As I stand there in the feet-spread-out, hands up, you're-*so*-going-to-prison pose, hindsight storms my mind. Had I not agreed to join the joyride excursion from our small college in the red-rock desert of southern Utah to Pipe

Spring National Monument; had I not blown off my classes (as I always did) along with the assigned reading in my creative writing class—in this case, Ed Abbey's *Desert Solitaire*—I wouldn't be here.

But I am, and there is nothing I can do to change it. So I stay quiet—too freaked out to say anything. But my friend, the one who was driving, is running his mouth: "You probably really get off busting people, don't you?" he says to the cop cuffing him.

"Only when I bust people like you," he says.

One of the police radios squawks. A desert gust lifts some dust and blows it into the road. A car passes and a little girl stares at me. We make eye contact. Her face a grainy, haunting film still. She's maybe five and I can only imagine what she must be thinking.

She's thinking: *bad guy.*

Soon, we're in the car. They're taking us in. The entire episode is surreal, and I can't quite process it because (1) I'm stoned and (2) I'm a scared-shitless boy flung into the sudden country of men and consequence. Things become more surreal as the squad car rolls into a sandy parking lot outside of a courthouse-cum-mobile home in Moccasin, Arizona. Inside, we are handcuffed to metal folding chairs in the living room. Cheap cream draperies hang down to the gray shag carpet, and the wood paneling darkens the room. The judge, who, evidently, is also a farmer, stomps in through the kitchen, removes his rubber irrigation boots, and sits before us at a card table in his tube socks. He's a paunchy man with thinning gray hair. An American flag and an Arizona state flag flank the rickety table. He shoves his glasses up the bridge of his nose and picks through some papers on the table before him. "Where'd you boys drive from?" he asks without looking up from the documents before him.

"Cedar City," my friend says miserably.

"We're students, there," I say, "at suu." This detail seems important to me, a detail that might suggest a different story. And yet, once I start speaking, my voice wanders apologetically.

"My grandson goes there," he says and looks up. He tells us his grandson's name and we're shocked and relieved because we actually know him, because we are in the same fraternity. It's a small and occasionally coincidental world, and we feel the weight lift a little.

"Possession of marijuana in the state of Arizona is a felony offense." He looks at us. It's unclear if it's a statement or a question, and because we're stoned and under arrest, we look at him blank faced, and nod.

He takes his glasses off, pockets them, and says, "Listen: in your case, I'm willing to drop it to a class-B misdemeanor." Then he adds some stiff lines about how if he ever sees us again, he will throw the book at us, and all the rest. And because we're boys, scared and stoned, we spew forth with all kinds of bobble-headed assurances, the whole, *We-sure-have-learned-our-lesson!* spiel.

In the end, we are fined four hundred dollars apiece and released on our own recognizance. The drive home is a long and sobering ride. We speak very little save some urgent promises that we will *never*—under *any fucking circumstances*—tell *anyone* (and that includes girlfriends, yo!) what had happened.

What happened in Moccasin stays the fuck in Moccasin.

Word.

That previous fall, I had fled my hometown of Soda Springs, Idaho, for Southern Utah University. It's beautiful country, and its beauty made attending class difficult. Plunk down the sagebrush-born, cow-shit-on-his-shoes, first-generation college kid in beautiful scenery inhabited by beautiful girls and be amazed that he ditches his classes. He doesn't know his ass from a hole in the sky because he is a nineteen-year-old boy who has confused the wondrous burdens of independence for manhood, or something like it.

He hasn't read *Desert Solitaire* and as a partial result, he'll fail the class. But instead of selling the book back like his classmates, he keeps it. Keeps it because he thinks he'll read it one day (and he will). He hangs onto it, too, because verdicts are falling like hammers from a dark sky. Academic transcript as verdict. Criminal record as verdict. Each of them adding up to the story of man he never dreamed of becoming. Keep the books. Hold on to the good stories.

It is easy now to see how frantic my desert isolations were, and how the dope and the booze and the girls helped to assuage the pains of the boy who wasn't yet man enough to name them.

Brinley, Bertrand R. *The Mad Scientists' Club.*
New York: Scholastic, 1965.

When I was eleven and in that sunset year of childhood
when it took actual concentration to discern the diaphanous line between daydreams and reality, when the stories
I read so fully colored my day-to-day loafing in rural Idaho
that I seldom knew where the page ended and the world
began, I picked up a particular book about a gang of goofy
kids whose lives I wanted to be my own so badly that it left
me aching in the joyous way books often leave us: high,
yet abandoned somehow. The feeling, when you have it,
is tactile and intoxicating. It is like love or victory or
surrender.

Set in the nostalgic and quaint town of Mammoth Falls,
The Mad Scientists' Club centers on a group of boy-geniuses
whose singular occupation was to hatch harebrained
schemes to save their town (or themselves) from one kind
of danger or another. Led by Jeff Crocker and the bespectacled Henry Mulligan (the main brain), the club met
daily in their headquarters, which was outfitted in the loft
of Jeff Crocker's barn. They had an in-house laboratory
complete with microscopes and vials of solutions and com-
pounds. They had telescopes. Transmitters. Tool boxes.
Plenty of books. And endless days to fill. It was a world that
to me felt actual, a realm whose cinematic stories stamped
my imagination, and I never wanted it to end.

So I formed my own Mad Scientists' Club. I enlisted five
of the smartest kids in my school. I secured a workspace

in the basement of the old hotel and café my family owned (plus I had claimed a stone clubhouse whose former life had been an aboveground root cellar). I bought a telescope (rather, I redeemed a shoebox filled with hundreds of my grandmother's cigarette coupons, which were enough to get the telescope from the Raleigh-Bel-Air merchandise catalog). I gathered tools, rope, pocket knives, drafting paper, pencils, protractors, a Commodore VIC-20, walkie-talkies, everything. We were in business. I called the meeting to order in the dank recesses of our basement, explained my intentions, my conception of what would surely be summer after summer of endless adventure. But the first meeting seemed forced and stilted.

"Like, what do you want to do?" a shaggy-haired kid asked.

"I'm bored," said another.

And another, who wrinkled his nose and waved his hand through the air, said, "Who beefed?"

In seconds, we all bolted from the table, toppling our chairs in the escape.

The attentions of eleven-year-old boys are often upended by that which is either sacred or profane, by either boobs or farts, or candy and cigarettes.

Ultimately, few if any of the ideas had legs, but the short list of agreed-upon projects looked something like this:

Build a small, unmanned rocket. We had started with some basic blueprints that involved an old water heater I salvaged from our basement, an oxygen tank my grandfather used on account of his emphysema, a sledgehammer, and a football helmet (for safety). The project, though, never got off the ground, so to speak.

Hack into the NORAD defense system mainframe using the Commodore VIC-20. We spent hours in front of the "computer"—a keyboard hooked into a television set—running any number of commands that would, we were sure, destabilize global defense centers everywhere. We typed words like NORAD and *missile* and *defense* and *top secret*, and for each entry we jabbed into the keyboard, the television screen spat back its unwavering response: SYNTAX ERROR.

Build a satellite that will intercept alien communications. I remember monkeying around with a coffee can, some parts from my Erector Set, and some speaker wire, but the project never lived past a crude prototype, and we never intercepted anything but an all-Spanish radio station (which was cool) and dust motes.

I was so taken with the club and its promising future that I bought T-shirts and had Mrs. Jensen at Keith's department store affix three felt iron-on letters—"M.S.C."—on each shirt. "They're for my club," I told her. "We're scientists," I said working my bubble gum. She smiled, nodded, rang up my order, and bagged my shirts. I unwadded some bills, got my receipt, and pumped my bike home through the summer air.

But nothing—not monogrammed T-shirts, not cloud-high ideas, or the books that inspired them—could prolong that age and that time, and soon the inevitability of girls or other tinseled distractions had eclipsed the Mad Scientists' Club, and that line between daydreaming and the actual world widened in a way that was both liberating and cruel.

The Children's Bible. Racine WI: Golden Press, 1965.

My family wasn't what you would call religious, but they weren't exactly irreligious either. Take for instance the time my parents gave me an illustrated copy of *The Children's Bible*. On its purchase, it became, and continued to be, the only Bible in our home, and I was the only one who sniffed around in its pages. Put another way, mine was a home where the expectations of the Christian faith were perfunctory at best, rather than practiced. If you lived up to those expectations, great. If not, great. Even my mother's reasoning for buying it felt pro-forma: "Every boy has to have a children's Bible." For whatever reason, I still have this book. I am not a religious man, and, as if fulfilling its ho-hum legacy, it remains the only Bible in my household. Little surprise, then, that it wears a kicked-around look. Its spine is blown off. Markered doodles blight the passages, and it reeks of my parents' cigarette smoke. On the inside dedication page it reads

To: Brandon
From: Mom & Dad
Christmas 1978.

That was when we lived for a brief period in Richland, Washington. Living out the story of boomers, job seekers, and fresh-starters in an antsy, post-Vietnam country, my stepdad, Bud, my mother, and I packed up our belongings and moved from Soda Springs, Idaho, and the hotel my grandparents owned (and we helped run), to West Richland—a desert town made plentiful by the Columbia River, and a settlement made complicated by the Hanford Nuclear Reactor, where my dad had found work as an electrician. This was 1976—two years before I received the Bible. I remember bits about the move, nothing more. I recall, for instance, the sun blazing on the car hood. It was a drive from one high-desert sage-brush plain to another. And I remember the long, curious shadow the car threw over the basalt ridges and coulees and how it played on the brush like a movie—flickering, animated.

I remember fragments from that time. On February 26, 1979, for instance, Dad said the word *eclipse*, as in a solar eclipse, and for a moment I was frightened. "The sun will disappear," he explained. "Behind the moon. We'll get to see it." My mother was excited, too, and between drags from her cigarette, she said that we were lucky. "Once in a lifetime event," she said. We turned the channel knob on our television set and all three news stations were abuzz with news of the total solar eclipse.

I remember asking if the sun would come back.

My parents laughed, beer cans in hand. "*No!*—it will vanish *forever!*" And then, correcting the sarcasm: "Of course it will, Bird-Turd." That was my dad's nickname for me: Bird-Turd. "Actually, it isn't going anywhere. Just looks like it is. Like an *optical illusion.*"

From Hanford, Dad brought home plates of dark glass, the kind of glass that was used in goggles and worn by military officials who witnessed the Trinity Test in 1945 in the New Mexico desert, the bomb born to the Manhattan Project, the Manhattan Project born at Hanford.

So there we were standing in ankle-high yellow grass in a junk-littered field in front of our squat clapboard rental, casting our eyes on this empyrean spectacle. "Careful now," Dad said. "Use the glass. Don't hurt your eyes."

Day had become night and night had become day as we stood in a shadow world beneath the eye of some God, that enormous black orb, retina flaring in the sky. And these three humans—mere stick-figures in the vast umbra of this event—watched breathless.

Dad patted me on the back. "There you go, pard. Can you see it?"

Pard. That was another name he gave me.

"I can see it," I said, craning my head toward the fiery ring, the great vanishing act above.

Because it was the 1970s, my parents liked to draw the curtains and lock the door in our rental so they could listen to the swampy romp of Credence Clearwater Revival and smoke from an enormous purple water bong without the neighbors peering in. Sometimes Dad would separate seeds and stems on white paper plates in the living room while I pushed toy trucks around on the red carpet and my mother cooked spaghetti in the small kitchen. The rules were very clear during such occasions: I was not to answer the door if someone knocked, nor could I pull back the curtain. Other times, they would invite their friends over and parties would roll from the afternoon into the evening and late into the night. And on Sunday mornings, while my mother and Dad nursed their hangovers (they would within a few years sober up completely), I would put on a beige polyester suit, grab my copy of *The Children's Bible*, and jump on a big white bus that rattled off to a Baptist church where everyone sang:

> Deep and wide
> Deep and wide,
> There's a fountain flowing deep and wide!

But when I returned in my wrinkled suit with *The Children's Bible*, the door would be locked, so I would knock and wait on the stoop like some vagabond child missionary dispatched to convert his unknown kin. *Come on*, I'd whisper. *Answer the door.* The neighbor kids would stare at me—and I would wave—and they were wondering, no doubt, why on earth I was locked out of my house—again. But it would take a few minutes for Dad to stash the water-bong and the paper plates and for my mother to light incense and clear the air. And then finally, the door would yawn open and the light of the day would flood the darkening living room and they would be all smiles. "Hey Pard!" Dad would call, glassy eyed, from the couch.

"How was church, kiddo?" My mother would ask.

And I'd shrug and run to my room to change into play clothes.

On a random day, about eight months after the total solar eclipse, I was standing in our lawn barefoot while a desert wind tugged at my T-shirt. It was spring. I heard what I took to be a distant sonic boom. Later, clouds, strange clouds, rolled over head, and it began to snow something that was not snow. The snow was something else, something dry. Cars stopped. People stepped out on their porches, hands visored to their foreheads, eyes sweeping the world. My neighbor snapped her clothes off the line. *What is it?* People asked. *It's ash*, they said. Fears abounded, if only for a few minutes, of Hanford, of war, of the worst possible thing. But it wasn't that. It was the mountain-turned-volcano to the north, Mount St. Helens. Within a day our yard was a beach of gray. Dad put me to work in the yard gathering ash into fruit jars, and my skin turned slate gray.

Everything felt big to me, epic almost, and I matched the changing world I saw outside to the pictures in *The Children's Bible*—pictures of flaming chariots racing through the skies, of Samson breaking the pillars, of Jesus walking on water. After studying those pictures, the notion of vanishing suns and exploding mountains began to make sense. You could expect the world to go crazy like that.

Clemens, Samuel Langhorne. *The Adventures of Huckleberry Finn.* Racine WI: Golden Press, 1965.

After *The Children's Bible* but before *The Mad Scientist's Club* there was *The Adventures of Huckleberry Finn.* I was ten years old and we were back in Soda Springs helping my grandparents run their hotel and café. It was the first time I read the story of Huck Finn, and I read the entire thing aloud to my grandmother and several women who worked in the café. While they hacked through heads of cabbage and diced boiled eggs, I read to them the topsy-turvy adventures of a boy I longed to be.

The spell it cast over me, if we are to call it such a thing, was so complete, so commanding, that it felt as though I had been born in the wrong era, mistakenly flung into modernity with no rope to lead me back to the world of antiquity, or "the olden times," as I called it then. The book's power I remember well. On summer afternoons, after an hour of reading, of stumbling across arcane passages and ripsaw dialects, I would snap the book shut and find myself outside and barefoot along the dampened banks of Soda Creek. I whittled spears from weeping willow branches and threw them, javelinlike, into the cold eddies of the creek, hoping for brook trout. I never speared a fish but it didn't matter. I was a boy and could not have been happier in that green part of the world I had carved out for myself. Upstream, two enormous weeping willows leaned across the creek from the lower bank on one side to the higher bank on the other. The tree trunks were bridges to be crossed, and a particular nook in one seemed ready-made to cradle the frame of a boy. And there I could lie and shut my eyes with the hypnotic gurgle of the stream swirling below me until something out of the ordinary wakened me from my boyhood slumber, something like a train whistle, a car horn, or, in some cases, the alarming surprise of a sudden erection. The latter would get me thinking of Huck Finn and whether or not he ever suffered from the involuntary boner. Certainly they had boners in the "olden times," but nowhere in the pages of the *Adventures of Huckleberry Finn* did I find any evidence of such a thing. Boys of a certain age spend too much time thinking about boners, it seems, in part because boys in that stage are too often ambushed by biology. They fall victim to some cruel joke of maturation. The one thing they are taught to control and conceal at all costs suddenly has a mind and agenda of its own. And in part because boys of that age just like saying the word *boner*. Once, my teacher was giving us the rundown on the suffix "-er" and how it meant "one who does" as in "farmer" (one who farms) and "worker" (one who works). So, what followed felt like a reflex, involuntary and spasmodic. I said it before I could unsay it: "Boner!—one who bones!"

"Schrand! Out!" The teacher barked. Before I knew it I was in the principal's office apologizing for offering what I took to be an apt example of the grammar lesson at hand.

Boys of that age are crammed into bodies they can't control. Your voice cracks without warning. Zits arrive overnight. Farts go off like landmines. You laugh at inappropriate times. It is an unpredictable mess made all the more cruel by the surprise erection. Consider for instance the day when you and your best friend are jumping on the neighbor girl's trampoline, giddy over the way her boobs surge up and down with the all the tramping and bouncing, and you realize with slasher-movie fright the serious error you have made in wearing soccer shorts. And so you swear off soccer shorts and trampolines especially when outfitted with boobed neighbor girls.

There are safer, less anxious places to reside.

Places like those described in the world of Huck Finn.

I saw his as a safe world, comprised of boys and men for the most part, a place where most of the men were boys themselves (like the Duke and Huck's father), and where the boys, of course, ached to be men. Caught in that heartbreaking paradox of both wanting to be a man and never wanting to leave childhood, Huck was a boy like me who yearned to be a man unlike his father. I sensed that in the book even at young age. Huck's world was unfettered by the anxieties of girls and rules and propriety. His was a green world into which he was born, and through which he passed on his raft, aging as he journeyed on. And part of me—the part that couldn't comprehend the biological stew that roiled within me—never wanted his river to end, never wanted him to find the dock of adulthood. If biology could be a cruel trickster to boys, then adulthood would be the cruelest of all.

Nor did I want my days along that creek to end, either. But somehow they did. Biology, if nothing else, ferried me into other reaches of my awakening world, and one day I simply forgot to go down into the lush stink of that creek bottom. Then one day became two days, and two became forever. Snap your fingers and it's gone.

Dickens, Charles. *Great Expectations.* New York: Bantam, 1982.

When my attentions eventually swung from the seriousness of the *Mad Scientists' Club* or the wonders of the creek bottom to the seriousness of girls and rock and roll, they swung with such force and biological thrust that I was electrified by the man who grew within and embarrassed by the boy I really was. Adolescence strikes boys like an earthquake or volcano—rumbling, unpredictable, and it is by turns both frightening and thrilling.

It was during these tremulous days that my English teacher, Ms. Tipton—an erudite woman with an occasional dramatic flair—assigned Dickens's *Great Expectations.* "Dickens is simply *wonderful,*" she chimed, swooping her arms through the air. "And this novel is no exception." While the A students beamed and nodded their heads, I shot rubber bands at a girl in jeans so tight they made me fidget in my seat. *Great Expectations* amounted to background noise in the great rhythmic song of hormonal uplift. The odds, then, that I would surrender to this story were unfavorable and had more to do with the girl in tight jeans and their effect on me than they did with the book itself. But when I learned that the protagonist's name was Pip, the book was over for me. "What the hell kind of name is *Pip?*" I shouted in the hallway after the bell rang.

"It's a douche bag name!" my friend Kenny called out over the crowd. Kenny was tall and fence post thin with spiky blond hair and had a slapstick way of contorting his lankiness to great comedic effect.

"Great Expectations, my ass," someone else complained.

"How about *No* Expectations," I said, and issued a smattering of high-fives.

The verdict was in. It was Game Over for Dickens and his lad, Pip. Evidently, the pitfalls of social climbing in early-nineteenth-century British society could not compete with what command-ed our interests during our biological quake: girls in tight jeans, keggers at Rendezvous Flats, and Mötley Crüe. Boys born in sagebrush don't go gently into the pages of Victorian literature. This much was clear.

I read maybe twenty pages of GE—and that is a big maybe. My eyes glazed over at names like Havisham and Bentley Drum-mle. If there was an exam, and I am sure there was, I likely failed it. I couldn't even make sense of Dickens. His was a dead, irrel-evant world. The language was off key and existed on a register that was out of reach, threatening, or emasculating even.

So while my other classmates—the beaming, college-bound crowd, those who didn't appear haunted by the pink promise of sex or anxious for Friday nights at Mud Lake—read their Dickens, I played guitar.

Our small school had only one independent rock band, and I was its rhythm guitarist. I had become a metal head, and al-most weekly, we came up with new band names: Terminal Clapp, Overdrive, Scab, The Rabid-Green Mosquito Vikings, and Un-derglass. The latter name, which we actually adopted, came from the mind of Steve, our bass player. "It's like Under-*Class*, but, you know, with *glass*—instead of class. Get it?"

"Yeah, I get it," I had said, though I didn't quite get it. I sub-scribed to the name, even if half-heartedly, because I figured his excitement over the name had to do with some cultural ref-erence I wasn't privy to. After all, Steve, while a full-blown rocker himself, what with the long curly hair, bracelets, Camaro, and Dio T-shirts, was an avid reader. If anyone in the band was privy to an obscure cultural reference, it was Steve.

If our band was always on the hunt for a new name or image, we were as equally pressed to find a place to practice, a steady place. Although I grew up in an enormous hotel with a bar and café, we couldn't practice there on account of driving away guests or customers with clunky Iron Maiden riffs or feedback. So I envisioned some kind of loft because that is what KISS had practiced in when they were starting out in Queens, New York, and the whole idea of practicing in a loft made my head tingle. When no one was around I would pretend to do interviews with *Rolling Stone* and *Hit Parader* and *Metal Edge*. "So, tell me, Brandon. Where did you guys begin? I mean before your meteoric rise to stardom?"

"Well, we started out in this loft . . ."

But Soda Springs didn't have any lofts that I knew of, and so we started asking local churches. We thought the LDS church would be a sure thing, but their rejection came as clear and loud as a slammed door. Eventually, the Catholic church let us practice in their basement. They gave us full rein. We could even keep our equipment there. And for months, we met up at the church after school and muddled through renditions of "Shout at the Devil," and AC/DC's "Highway to Hell."

One day after practice, while we coiled cords and snapped shut our gear cases, Steve handed me a book. "Dude," he said, while hooking a lock of hair behind his ear. "Check this shit out. It's fucking *great*."

It was called *Rock 'n' Roll Nights* by Todd Strasser, and Steve had checked it out from our school library. The cover featured an illustration of a rock band on stage: a hot, sultry blonde in a spaghetti-strap red dress on bass; a guy in a straightjacket on vocals; another guy in coattails on keyboards, and a burn-out on drums. "Cool," I said.

Steve took it back. "I'll finish it tonight. You definitely need to read it."

Shortly afterward, I was browsing the YA section in the library and pulled it from the shelves. That night I started reading and didn't put it down. Gary Specter, the protagonist, was seventeen, about my age, and fronted their band, Gary Specter and the Electric Outlet. It was by turns a wholesome and dirty read. It was wholesome in that Gary was not the stereotypical rocker who shirked school for rock and roll. "For one week Gary forgot about music and concentrated on school," Strasser writes. "For his final project in poetry writing he handed in the lyrics of all the songs he'd written that year, and his term paper for music history compared the musical development of Mozart with that of John Lennon." It was dirty, too, in that the book opens with Gary waking in a girl's bed but when she tries to mount him, he stops her cold: "I don't love you," he says. It was an unexpectedly wholesome turn on an otherwise dirty scene, and I would be lying if I didn't say I felt cheated, yet compelled to read more.

But it was dirty, still, because Susan—the sultry blonde bass player—was cool and edgy and flirtatious, and I was into her. And so was Gary. Sort of. Trouble there is, Susan and Gary were first cousins. At one point in their younger years, they had gotten tipsy and started fooling around under a blanket, and I recall that scene as both disturbing and deliriously arousing. And even though that was their only sexual encounter, it haunted their relationship through the rest of the book.

Like me, or Huck Finn, Gary Specter was two parts boy, and one part man. He was fever-sick with the great expectations of becoming a rock star and was subject to the fledgling sexual electricity that arced through his body. In other words, Gary Specter was real (unlike Pip). He felt actual to me, like someone I could have hung around with, like someone whose band I would have joined. I felt his joy at hearing his song "Rock Therapy" play over the radio for the first time; his tumult for his one-time brush with his hot cousin; and his anxiety of losing gigs to the rival band—Johnny Fantasy and the Zoomies.

Little surprise then that *Rock 'n Roll Nights* took the place of *Great Expectations,* and it did so for all of the obvious reasons. When I wasn't practicing my guitar riffs for an upcoming gig, I didn't "concentrate on school," as Gary Specter had. Instead, I was lost in the pages of *Rock 'n Roll Nights* and those pages alone.

Then one night while lying in bed fantasizing about Susan or the girl in tight jeans in my English class, I realized that my ears would turn red hot whenever I masturbated. They typically turned red when I was nervous or anxious, and like Gary Specter (or Pip, for that matter), I had my own anxieties during those uneven days. But I hadn't before connected masturbation with this strange expression, and so I was worried. While I replayed the film in my head of the girl in tight jeans, and how those jeans revealed in startling detail the lush contours of the secret female body, or about Susan and her curvy, sultry ways, my ears shot red and thrummed with blood. Soon the paranoia crept in. What if everyone but me knew the tell-tale giveaway for masturbation? What if red ears were the twin beacons—the scarlet satellites—that announced shame and personal defilement? So there I lay perfectly still, blinking in the dark. My ears were so hot I thought they could light the room. After that, whenever my ears turned red in public, my heart knocked around in my chest. *Everyone here thinks I've been doing The Dirty*, I'd think. I feared awkward social situations where someone might say, "Why are your ears red?" And I might respond, "I don't know. It's not like I've been masturbating."

Short of seeking a doctor's advice, there was really no one or no source to turn to in such matters. I lived in Soda Springs, Idaho, before the Internet. Our isolations were palpable and definitive. I knew no more about my interior world than I did the outside world. It was 1989—a few steps into my sophomore year—and out there, somewhere, was something called the Cold War. Occasionally, I would hear the phrase Iran-Contra scandal. Closer to home a farm crisis loomed, but even that was abstract, and the only concrete thing I could associate with it was the closing of the bank across the street. I remember peering through their dark glass windows one afternoon only to see a ghosted office space with boxes here and there, severed phone cords, and an overstuffed trash can. So I knew nothing or next to nothing about the world or my biology, and had, as a result of my isolations, few resources to turn to. My family owned encyclopedias, but only three volumes: H, R, and W. While I had learned loads about Hypothalamus, Radon, and Warthogs, there existed real and panicky gaps in my knowledge of the alphabetized world generally, and more specifically, of Ears and Masturbation. It is not a stretch, then, to say that these gaps made me feel all the more isolated from the world, and all the more removed from the college-bound crowd who no doubt possessed entire sets of encyclopedias. Mine wasn't a home that needed (or, more to the point, could afford) a set of *Funk & Wagnall's.*

Like so many boys of that age who are all astir over the sexual storm inside and the imminent yet abstract future outside, I was desperate to find a book that would unmask the real me. And I was convinced that *Great Expectations* wasn't it. I would never have allowed myself to identify with Pip or anyone walking around in Dickens's novel even though I had a lot in common with Pip. Moreover, I failed to draw the connections between Pip and Gary, to see their commonalities despite their being worlds and centuries apart. Each wanted desperately to climb high walls. And when given the chance, each risked the trappings of a cruel world dressed in niceties. The expectations of Pip said that he could never ascend; of course he did ascend the social strata, but only at a cost. The expectations of Gary said that he would never make it as a rock star, though he did, or so we are led to believe by the end of the novel. And Gary and Pip each maintained complicated relationships with women. Even if I had drawn those connections, I am uncertain as to whether such a revelation would have quelled the squall I felt inside. There is the off chance that I wouldn't have felt so alone in the well of my uncertainties, and that might have helped.

Other factors— factors beyond my control—helped to magnify my isolations and anxieties. Early in my junior year, for instance, Mr. Jepsen, the school counselor, a quirky, smart, and balding bachelor who donned an on-the-job smile, made—to my thinking—a surprise visit to my history class to discuss scholarships.

He went on at length about this scholarship and that scholarship, each of them earmarked for those boasting at least a 3.5 GPA or better, usually better. I sat in the back with my long, stringy, bleach-blond hair, a dangly skull earring, sunglasses, and a Harley-Davison headband à la Axl Rose, listening. At the close of his presentation, Mr. Jepsen called for questions.

"Yo!" I yoed.

"Mr. Schrand."

"What if like you don't have all those grades and still like want to go to college? Like, what about the C students?"

"*You*," he said, snapping his binder shut, "should have thought about *that* three years ago."

The class whoaed and someone said, "Burn!"

It was an accurate if cold verdict, made icier by the public spectacle of it all. Of course he was right. But it felt like I had been forced to sit on the boundary of a discussion I had no place in. I didn't even know the language. College was what other people did. Scholarships had everything to do with the great expectations of the college-bound crowd and not the rocker kid who had been chucked from class for yelling "boner" during a suffix lesson. And so I felt sorry for myself.

By the time Ms. Tipton called for our copies of *Great Expectations* to be turned in, I had finished reading Strasser's book. I returned it to the library with some reluctance. Then about a week later, I did the strangest thing. I found myself in the library wasting time in the YA section, and when the librarian took a phone call, I pulled *Rock 'n Roll Nights* from the shelf, slipped it into my duffle, and ducked out. Why I felt the need to steal that book is beyond me. I still have it to this day. Inside, the card pocket is stamped with a dozen due dates. The last two are APR 23 1990 and MAY 07 1990—the dates Steve and I checked them out, respectively. The adult within me thinks it would be a good idea to return it to the library even after all these years, but the boy in me can't fathom of letting it go.

Emerson, Ralph Waldo. *Essays of Ralph Waldo Emerson.* Introduction by Carl Van Doren. New York: Literary Classics, 1945.

I had decided to go to college on a lark at the urging of my friends rather than my family. Originally, I had been content with the shimmering daydream of becoming a rock star. All throughout my childhood—from the raucous days in West Richland, where I heard my first KISS song ("Calling Dr. Love"), to Soda Springs, where my bedroom was plastered with metal posters cut from *Rolling Stone, RIP, Hit Parader,* and *Metal Edge*—music was my sanctuary. I would read those magazines cover to cover, too, before stripping them of the concert photos of Dokken, Van Halen, or Ratt. So in this way, college was never an option. I had only the vaguest idea of what college even was. All I knew of college was that it was far away and expensive.

And that it wasn't for guys like me.

My insides were all astir over my future. I was divided not just between the boy inside and the man I was turning into, but between my role as rocker and someone who wanted to be taken seriously. Because mine was a small school (I graduated with sixty-five or so students), social cliques were by and large penetrable, if one chose to penetrate them. And I did. Ours wasn't a world like Pip's, in other words. So I occupied contradictory territory. I drank beer with the rockers on weekends at keggers down by Bear River, but skateboarded with the Mormon kids on weeknights. I was voted both class "space cadet" and, later, student body vice president (no big feat, really, in such a small pond).

But the more nights I spent with the Mormon kids skating around their church parking lot, the more our conversations trailed into the topic of college. And the more weekends I spent chugging beer and belching with the rocker crowd, the more the conversations tilted toward the topic of finding a job. Two roads emerged, as it were, and it was becoming clear which one I would take.

When I announced to my parents that I wanted to go to college, their response wasn't anything like I had imagined it to be. I thought they would be thrilled, jubilant, and would exhaust themselves in the fever of the good news. I thought they would make cakes and place telephone calls to far-flung relatives. Instead, they felt ambushed. I was in my senior year and only now had I mentioned college. Most parents in that broad economic band we call the middle-class have these discussions early on, when their children are still olive-sized in the womb. Strangely, we hadn't really discussed my future in any substantive way. A generational, familial (and to some extent, cultural-demographic) pattern was in place that unraveled the need for such sit-down, kitchen-table discussions, and that pattern looked something like this:

1. Go to school (school here meaning elementary and secondary school).
2. Graduate from school.
   a. Or don't graduate from school.
3. Get a job (agricultural, or, more typically, at one of the mines in town).
4. Stay with that job.
   a. Or don't stay with that job either by way of firing (unacceptable), quitting (frowned upon), or layoff (common in a town like Soda Springs).
   b. Get a new job, etc., and repeat a & b until you do stay with one job.
5. Get married.

6. Find a place (usually a trailer to begin, then upgrade to a modular, rambler, postwar home, etc.).
7. Have kids.
8. Retire.

The assumption, I guess, was that I would simply take to the currents of that pattern as easily as one takes to sleep and the ebb of dreams that follows. And to be completely honest, I had at one point craved that pattern of what I called "normal." I had been in that all-too-familiar teenage crisis where I wanted a normal life. I lived in a hotel, not a house. I ate in a café, not a dining room. I had a parking lot, not a yard. So when I visited my friends' modular, rambler, or postwar homes and their savory kitchen scents and their green lawns and their musty garages, I ached to be a part of it. I wanted what they had. (The irony here, of course, is that all my friends wanted to live in a hotel, eat in a café, and ride around a parking lot on their bike and have no lawn to mow.) The closer I got to graduation, however, the more I ached for a different dream, one that cast me far away from the generational pattern. Let me be clear here, though. There isn't anything wrong with the pattern I listed above. What I call a pattern, others call the American Dream, and it may well be. In fact, I am sure it is for a great many people. But I wanted to break the pattern because while it existed as a dream for some, it had morphed into something of a nightmare for me. I wanted new dreams, the ones I got from books.

It was on a bright afternoon that I recall pushing through the door and announcing to my parents that I wanted to go to college. Correction: I said that I *was going* to college, as if the decision had already been finalized in their absence. Moreover, they would have to write the check.

My mother sat at the tiny kitchen table with a cigarette in her hand. Her long dark hair had a few faint gray streaks in it. She parked her cigarette on the ashtray, removed her glasses, and cleaned them on the tail of her shirt. "And just how do you think we can afford this?"

I wasn't sure. So I shrugged, fished a soda from the fridge and said, "We'll just have to figure it out. Because I'm going."

"Funny, I don't recall you mentioning college until this very moment."

My dad materialized from the backyard in his standard uniform: flannel shirt, suspenders, jeans, work boots, and his IBEW (International Brotherhood of Electrical Workers) hat.

My mother and I were silent. He filled his IBEW mug with tap water and asked what was going on.

"I'm going to college," I announced.

"You flipping the bill?"

"No. You guys will have to cover it. But look: I need this. It's crucial. I mean, I *have* to get out of this place."

"And you just decided this now?" He said.

"Yeah. More or less."

"I'm not going to shell out on something that just crossed your mind, pard. Sorry, but that's life."

"Why don't you work for a year or two, then see how you feel about it," my mother offered.

"I have to leave now, like ASAP. Or I will die here!" My tone was sharp and alarmist.

"Then don't let the door hit you in the ass on the way out," my dad said, his tone sharpening in proportion to my own.

"So ISU?" My mother said and took a drag from her cigarette. She meant Idaho State University, the college in Pocatello, fifty-four miles west.

"No. Absolutely not."

"Why not? You could live here and commute. See if you like it. Get a part time job."

"What part of leaving are you not getting here?"

"You don't even like school," she said.

"It beats the shit out of staying here and working in the mines. Jesus, I can't believe we're arguing about this! Most parents would be thrilled. Not you! Oh, no!"

"Do you even realize what you are asking of us?"

"I. Fucking. Need this. If I don't get out, I. Will. Fucking. Die."

"Watch your mouth," my mother snapped.

"You've lived your lives. Now let me live mine!"

"Fuck you," my dad said.

"He didn't mean it like that," my mother said, and twisted her cigarette into the amber glass of the ashtray.

I hung my head and mumbled an apology. The room went silent. My dad disappeared into the backyard.

And finally, I said, "Grandma said she would pay for it, if you wouldn't." This was true. But pride alone wouldn't allow my mother to let her mom pay for my tuition. So in this way, her hand was forced. And they agreed with some grave reluctance.

Of course I didn't consider what a great burden my ambush had been on them, financially. I didn't consider their own struggles at the time, their own fight to keep the expense column from eclipsing the income column. I didn't consider intangibles like their fears and concerns, like why their son, who skated through school on a C average, all of a sudden wanted to enroll at a four-year university, or how they must have worried that I would certainly fail, and so on.

Part of what edged me toward the college decision was my involvement with the theater crowd. It wasn't much of a crowd, really. It was six students and Ms. Tipton, our English teacher who served as our advisor. I acted in plays like *The Miracle Worker*, *Lil' Abner*, *The Night of January 14th*, and even played Bob Cratchit in Dickens's *A Christmas Carol*. (Apparently, I had had a change of heart when it came to Dickens). I had even spent a late night writing my own comic play, which I later produced and staged in front of the school. Titled "Therapy Group," the play involved a cast of screwball patients and a therapist, who himself was trying to cope with being a therapist of such screwballs. I borrowed the play whole cloth from a radio play that had aired one night in the previous weeks. It also borrowed heavily from the old *Bob Newhart Show*, which I used to watch with my mother and dad when we lived in West Richland. I changed the characters and their wacky traits, but outside that, it is fair to say that it was full-throttled, unapologetic plagiarism. The play, however, went over well and caught the attention of my teacher, Ms. Tipton. "You have talent," she told me one day. "Real talent."

The twisted part is that I believed her. I had started to convince myself that I had actually written the play. "She's right," I remember thinking. "I *am* good!"

The daydream I created and that she validated had me in center stage as some kind of budding theater impresario. I am tempted to say I needed that kind of validation no matter the ethical cost, and because no real harm came from my fraud (no one died, for instance), that play was a first rung on some great Dickensian ladder I aimed to climb.

And so it was the best of times. I was playing in a band, acting on stage, and writing. Girls started to pay attention to me, even more so than before. I was living a daydream, and I was its author. At night I would write comedy sketches and practice in front of my mirror in my bedroom. Once, at an impromptu theater competition in the neighboring town, our team was struggling. I had to go up against a gorgeous girl who had all night long commanded the stage, what with her rapier wit, machine-gun tongue, and Cinemax boobs. The judge read off a scenario we had to act in (something about walking through a cemetery), and I pulled out all my comedy sketches, one after another, twisting and forming them, however improbably, to fit the scenario. In moments I had reclaimed the stage, and the audience ruled in our favor. We won. Ms. Tipton was thrilled.

The girl approached me moments later with her hand extended. "Congratulations," she said. "You were *fantastic!*" She was a commanding presence even off stage and I was mildly aroused by her long dark hair, olive skin, red lips, and abyssal eyes.

"But you were great, too!" My attempt to leaven the praise rang false and I tried to make up for it by cracking some lame self-deprecating joke. She stood before me with those gathering eyes, smiled, then spun around and dashed off to greet a friend with open arms, her booming voice full of song as if the two hadn't seen each other in years.

"Relax," my friend, Keith said. "She's mission-bound. No one's getting her."

I knew what that meant. She was going on a Mormon mission, so I felt the quick daggers of defeat undo the fantasy before it ever got a chance to form.

Keith was a tall, wry kid with Buddy Holly hair who, for many years in school, I took to be a momma's boy. He was soft spoken and nerdish in elementary school, so I never paid much attention to him. But in high school he found some inner confidence that pulled girls into his orbit like some centrifugal force, and I began to take note. He was one of the six theater students and we started hanging out, watching movies at his house, and hitting all the dances. He was a good Mormon kid who was looking for love and heavy petting, and I was looking for sex (though at the time I thought we were looking for the same thing), but we got along well enough. On Friday nights we co-hosted a radio show on KBRV–KFIS Soda Springs, called—unimaginatively—the Keith and Brandon Show. All I recall from the radio show is that we opened and closed it with Booker T. and the M.G.'s "Green Onions," and we took requests from the six or seven fourth-graders who tuned in to listen. On Sundays I ran the radio station myself and spent hours there playing the required repertoire: the Lutheran Hour, the Mormon Tabernacle Choir, public service announcements (PSAs), and some weather spots. Otherwise, I read. And the one book I kept taking to the station with me was Emerson's *Essays*.

It was an uphill read, but I was committed if nothing else. I was graduating in two months and I wanted to make up for four years of Cs. I tackled "Self-Reliance" first and understood very little, I'm sure. Some of it I did understand, however, and underlined passages while lying flat on my back in the radio station: "Your genuine action will explain itself, and will explain your other genuine actions. Your conformity explains nothing. Act singly, and what you have already done singly will justify you now. Greatness appeals to the future." Parts of Emerson—parts like these that I underlined—made a lot of sense and was good stuff for a kid looking to graduate and climb Dickensian walls. His aphoristic style was easy to digest in pieces. Other lines both excited and frustrated me: "Our language is mendicant and sycophantic." That was less easy to digest but thrilling because I had picked up two new words that were fun to say—mendicant and sycophantic—and, not unlike a boy learning a new swear word, I would wedge them awkwardly into casual conversations with girls in hopes that my stunning vocabulary would lead to sex.

Oh, high school sex. What could be more mind-blowing and tragic all at the same time? Girls and boys who grow up in the hinterlands of rural America are cursed by hunger and isolation. You are cut off from everything and everyone, and television only makes the greater world more, not less, abstract. There is no Internet. There is no cell phone. No Facebook, no Myspace, no Twitter, no Kindle. It's the late 1980s and all you've got is a rotary phone and a Spark-o-matic tape-deck and hormones and all the time in the world.

So you find yourself logging your hour at the library desk, which is part of your responsibilities as the librarian's teaching assistant. Also helping the librarian is this hot little honey with whom you have been flirting for weeks, and on one quiet afternoon when the library is deserted she sidles up to you and puts her hand on your stomach and then slides it down to the fun zone, and says, "What are you doing for lunch?"

If you were cool and smart, you would purr in her ear something obvious like, "*You.*" But you're not that cool and smart, or at least that quick, and because her hand is on you and your face shoots red and you start blinking, and what you finally say is, "Where do you want to go?"

So you drive out to this little park north of town, and during the entire drive (which is only five minutes but feels like you will never, *ever* get there), you think the buttons on your Levis might pop at any minute. She is looking through your tape case scoping out your Ozzy and Def Leppard and Cinderella cassettes, all the while snapping her gum and shooting you *fuck-me* looks, and you'll be lucky if you don't wreck your yellow 1979 Ford Courier right into the goddamn ditch. But you keep it on the road and roll into the parking lot of the park—which, and thank God, is empty. It's under a full blue sky, that you walk behind the pavilion and start making out and grabbing handfuls of goodies, and eventually, you hump right there in the grass. First she's on top and then says, "I like to be on bottom," and with great awkwardness, you swap-out, and go to work because she's all hot and blonde and dirty and wears way too much perfume and chews Bubbalicious, and she's moaning and chewing her gum and you could die right there in the grass.

And still you go! But little annoying thoughts flash through your mind while your are living the dream, thoughts like *What if someone sees us?* And *Should I be wearing a rubber?* And *Is she on the pill?* But these are silly annoyances in the midst of such American glory, and you toss those idiot thoughts like yesterday's mail.

The entire opera of rural hunger and isolation and humping in the park is over in like seventy seconds. If you had a cigarette, you'd suck it down baby, but you don't, and so she offers you some watermelon Bubbalicious, and that's good enough, by god. Couldn't be any better.

After school, when your mother asks, "How was school today?" You'll shrug and say, "It was good," by which you mean LIKE TO-TALLY FUCKING AWESOME!

Because it is high school and because hunger and isolation are the twin devils of madness in your sagebrush world, you find yourself again in the midst of this delicious tragedy, parked at the edge of town at Piss Holler (named so because it's where, after dragging Main Street, you go to piss and holler), listening to Whitesnake. The colored lights of your equalizer (or EQ) wink in the dark. The girl in the tight jeans from English class has freed you from your own tight jeans and is down there making slurping sounds while your body jerks and convulses and you stomp the floor and the brake pedal and the red glow of the brake lights illuminate in spasmodic pulses the grain silos next to the railroad tracks, and oh, my God!

Whitesnake fucking rocks!

There was in those lusty days a frenzied period in which I still hadn't settled on *which* college to attend. Time was running out. All my college-bound friends had everything figured out, as if college had been in the plans all along, which, of course, it had. My decision was as new as dawn. Originally, I had considered the University of Idaho, but my SAT scores were as unimpressive as my grades, and I feared I wouldn't meet their benchmark. Then I had considered Boise State, but after a visit, it felt commuterish and sprawly. Finally, the decision came to me one night at a party. I use the term *party* here loosely as it consisted of Mormon kids sitting around someone's living room telling cornball jokes while that someone's mother (I forget who) shuttled in and out with batches of cookies and caffeine-free soft drinks and other little plattered goodies. I was there because I wanted to fit in, but also—strangely—because I had hoped to have sex. (As a side note, you should know that I had been baptized into the Mormon Church just a year earlier because, again, I thought the road to a particular girl ran through the Mormon Temple. I suffered from a bizarre disconnect wherein my secular daydreams didn't even come close to matching the ecumenical realities (i.e., fornication = sin) on the ground.)

But I was also at the party because Keith had dragged me along (he had hoped to score some heavy petting). At some point toward the later hours of the evening, the conversation turned once again to the college question. Two-thirds were heading off to Brigham Young University, or its smaller sister school, Ricks College (now BYU-Idaho). Others were going to Idaho State University in Pocatello. A couple were enrolled at the University of Idaho. My friend, Heidi, however, was going to Southern Utah University. She wanted to become (and indeed did become) a choreographer. "They have a great theater program there. You should come with me." And just like that, I agreed. Turns out, her aunt worked in financial aid, and arranged an out-of-state fee waiver on the fly, and I was in. I hadn't so much as seen a postcard of the campus, and already I was packing.

In all, I packed eight books in my trunk for college. Here's the list, in no particular order: 1. Richard Adams's *Watership Down*. It was assigned reading in my senior English class, and though I wouldn't admit it to anyone, I loved the book. (*If you can write about rabbits*, I remember thinking, *well shit, you can write about anything*.) 2. Jim Morrison's *American Night*. 3. Morrison's *Wilderness*. 4. And yes, Morrison's *Lords and the New Creatures*. I was obsessed, obviously, with The Doors. 5. *The Portable Machiavelli*. Before heading off to college, I had asked a friend who was a year ahead of me what I should read before arriving on campus. He was tall and thin and slightly effeminate (I remember puzzling over his infatuation with Janet Jackson, for instance) and smart. He seemed, too, well, sophisticated, or as sophisticated as one can be coming from Soda Springs. "You should read 'The Prince,' by Machiavelli," he said. I pulled a receipt from my Velcro Metallica wallet—classy because it read "Metal Up Your Ass"—and scribbled the title down. "And Aristotle. And Plato. And Dante. And Milton. And . . ." At the end of it, I had lists on three crumpled receipts. Three lists that would save me. So I carefully folded them back into my Metallica wallet, and said, "Bitchin'." He laughed and we parted ways. I planned a trip to the nearest bookstore, fifty-four miles northwest to Pocatello (or 108 miles round trip). 6. Hunter Thompson's *Fear and Loathing in Las Vegas*. It was a beat-to-shit copy and was missing its cover. I had it on extended (read: permanent) loan from Steve, our band's bassist. "Fucking best book I have ever read," he said, hooking a lock of hair behind his ear. Jangly sets of bracelets gleamed from both his wrists. "Here: read the first line," he said, all fidgety with excitement. I read it and felt at once amused and confused.

"It's a novel?" I asked.

"No, dude. It's Thompson!"

"So it's nonfiction?"

"It's *Thooooompson*, dude. Just read it."

I put it on my to-read list for college. 7. Mark Twain's *Life on the Mississippi*. As much as I loved my Golden Illustrated volumes of Huck Finn and Tom Sawyer, I knew better than to bring "kid books" to college. So, I brought *Life on the Mississippi*. My mother had bought it for me because I was such a Twain fan. But I never really got into the book, and figured if I ever would, it would happen away at school. 8. The final book was Emerson's *Essays*. It was the oldest book in the collection and I can't remember how I came to own it, exactly. I liked it because it was old, and when I handled it, I would pretend I was smart. I daydreamed about reading the entire thing, cover to cover. I envisioned my dorm room to be all dark wood, a place to lose oneself in pages such as those in *Essays*.

I couldn't wait to get there.

Fitzgerald, F. Scott. *The Great Gatsby*. New York: Macmillan, 1992.

When I checked into my dorm room on the small campus of Southern Utah University, dragging my trunk and its eight books behind, I felt as though every detail about me, from my long hair, my trunk, my skateboarding shoes, the Delaware-sized hickey on my neck a girl had planted on me the night before I left, my Metallica tapes (yes—*tapes!*), to the way I talked and carried myself, betrayed who I was: working class kid from Skidmark, U.S.A. Inside, the room was wonderful and unremarkable. Wonderful because it was my room and because I was in college. Wonderful, too, because I was in college! And oh, my God! I was in college! And the twin bed and the desk and the drawers and the closet and the window and the curtains, and all of it was wonderful and crazy and it was all mine (or at least half of it; the left-hand side of the room). Wonderful, still, because the right hand side of the room, which had already been claimed, though my roommate was nowhere to be found, boasted a Red Hot Chili Peppers poster (the one with the socks on their johnsons), a Fugazi poster (who the hell was Fugazi?), and a Hüsker Dü poster (who?). It was unremarkable though because it was small and not paneled in dark wood as I had imagined. The walls were white cinderblock. The carpet, blue. The curtains, cream. Florescent lighting. But in the battle between the wondrous and the unremarkable, the wondrous won. Outside, the lawns sprawled across the grounds, and in the distance I could see the red-rock mountains of the southern Utah desert landscape. Gone were the drab basalt flows I had known as a kid growing up in southern Idaho. Gone was the brown earth. Here even the dirt was new. The whole world had changed down to the very soil I walked on.

I dropped my trunk and unrolled a huge Jane's Addiction poster, which I slapped on the wall above my bed. Just then the door swung open.

"You must be Brandon."

I was standing on my bed and jumped off. "Yeah." Recalling the two cute (read: lame) construction paper frogs (frogs? WTF?) taped to our door with our names on them, I said, "Mark, right?"

"I guess that makes us mates, yeah?"

Mates. He wasn't Australian. He was something else, something cooler.

Mark shut the door and fished two beers from a duffle on his bed. "What say we christen this place properly, yeah?" His tone was conspiratorial, and I was down. We bumped the lukewarm beer cans together and chugged.

Contents of my big red trunk other than the Eight Books:

1. Cassette tape carrying case featuring Metallica (numerous, as mentioned), KISS (old school and compilations), Faster Pussycat, Jane's Addiction, David Bowie, Howard Jones, The Cure, The Cult, Jesus Jones, EMF, Led Zeppelin, Steve Miller, The Eagles, The Doors, and others.
2. A turquoise fanny pack (I have no idea why).
3. Flowery bed sheets my mother sent me to college with.
4. Pink towels my mother sent me to college with . . . First, I am not sure what she was thinking. She didn't shop for new stuff like most parents do when sending their kids off to college. She just grabbed shit around the house we never used, like the pink fluffy towels, for instance, and the flowery bed sheets. Second, I have no idea what I was thinking in taking this stuff to college. Shouldn't pink towels and flowery sheets raise some alarms for most

people? How can a kid with long rocker hair and a penchant for Metallica not see where Ride the Lightning ends and the pink fluffy towels begin? How can he not see the disconnect? Where, O, where was the protest?

5. Flowery comforter. Egad. This is painful to write. But, yes, there was a poofy, whitish comforter with delicate flowers reaching here and there across its folds—a filigree of wretchedness.

6. A turquoise B.U.M. Equipment hat. Velcro back-strap and a really long bill.

7. Two high school yearbooks. Very embarrassing. Very painful to write. But yes, technically, I packed ten books. Taking high school year books to college was tantamount to taking your letterman's jacket (and believe me, had I lettered in anything worthy of earning a jacket, I would have packed the sucker in the Trunk of Embarrassment).

8. Coat and snow pants. Not so embarrassing except that my coat was fluorescent yellow with pink trim. The coat matched (embarrassingly) my Look Lamar snowboard, which was also florescent yellow with . . . pink . . . trim. Hang on a second. There is a pattern of pinkishness here. First, in my defense, this was 1991. I had just emerged from the 1980s, and I had been a rocker. Male rock stars looked like females (consider the argument my friends and I had when first seeing the cover of Poison's *Look What the Cat Dragged In*: "They're chicks!" "They're dudes!" "Chicks!" "Dudes!" And so on). Dudes wore pink all the time (witness Vince Neil circa Theater of Pain tour). Second, why am I getting so defensive about this?

9. Oakley sunglasses.

10. An extra SWATCH that had, you guessed it, a pink wrist band. Once you open the Trunk of Embarrassment, there's just no slamming it shut.

In many ways, Mark was the ideal roommate. At least for me. He was a non-practicing Catholic (that I didn't get stuck with a

Mormon roommate in Mormon country was nothing short of miraculous) who came from money, or at least a hell of a lot more than I came from. His father made a small fortune in the carpet business having specialized in the ornate Axminster carpets—floor coverings that date back to middle-eighteenth-century England. And adorning our dorm-room floor was none other than an Axminster rug. Beyond the money, though, Mark was simply more savvy than I was in almost all aspects of the world, and to this end, I had become something of a project to him. He looked worldly, too, and for good reason. His mother was a striking Latina, and his father was from England. So his Benjamin Bratt looks, brazen confidence, and joke-in-hand manner devastated girls. He became the most popular, and later, most notorious, guy not only in Hallway c of Juniper Hall, but of the entire complex. And I became Mark's Roommate, as in "Oh, you're Mark's Roommate" or "Pleased to meet you. I'm Mark's Roommate." His was a world of one continuous party. "Sky's the limit, mate," he was fond of saying. Life was a big laugh. If you weren't having a good time, you were taking up space. He was no jock, but if called on the court or into the field, he held his own and then some, which was more than I could say for myself. He skied, biked, SCUBA dived, golfed, and traveled. And he exercised no restraint in spending money. Sunglasses, cocktails, cigarettes, and the right music for any occasion (he would play James Bond soundtracks while having sex, reasoning that "the Betties think it's weird at first, but then they get into it"). It was no surprise, then, that Mark got to cue up the Bond tunes the first week of school.

I learned as much or more from Mark than I did from any of my classes during the first term. He taught me, for example, how to dress. This was no small thing. I looked like a bad accident of cultural collision. Hideous beyond hideous. Consider, for instance, the mustard-colored M.C. Hammer-type suit (with puffy shoulders) I wore with a black rayon shirt emblazoned with mustardy palm trees, a mustard tie, and a black plastic belt. What's worse is that I bought it at a store called Jeans West in the Pocatello Mall for five dollars plus tax. With my hair slicked back into a ponytail, I wore a five-dollar mustard suit with puffy shoulders and—here's the kicker—evidently thought it was *okay*, if not downright cool. But the first morning I donned the puffy mustard fiasco to my humanities class, I was set straight on just how ridiculous I looked. When class let out, I filed into the foyer of the brick English building where the bustle of students slowed in a snickery mass to observe the mustardy pony-tailed bonerific clown clomping back to his dorm in his black plastic penny loafers. Red-faced and humiliated, I burned a path straight to C-219 of Juniper Hall where, in a ceremonious huff of reinvention, I emptied my closet of anything that was pink, turquoise, mustard, puffy, flowery, jewely, or otherwise unacceptable. I filled my Army surplus duffle bag with what amounted to two-thirds of my total wardrobe and bolted down the stairs to the back parking lot where I dumpstered all the personal effects of the old me. That afternoon, I caught a ride to the only clothing store in our small college town and solemnly charged $300.00 to my ShittyBank 30% interest-rate credit card (a move that flew in the face of my frugal upbringing, which was its own kind of rebellion). But three hundred bucks didn't go far, as you can imagine, and so Mark offered to let me wear some of his clothes, an offer I abused at once.

The new me wore polo shirts and rugby shirts and Gap jeans and Vision Street Wear shoes (which I had retained). I also kicked around in a pair of Mark's cordovan low-top Doc Martens (shoes, I am ashamed to admit, I never returned to Mark). The new me started to see things more clearly. I had gotten away with wearing such clothes in small-town Idaho because it was small-town Idaho, but also because I was a class clown, and if my clothes were ridiculous (as they most often were), then they were just part of the act. People dismissed my get-ups out of hand: "Oh, that's just Brandon." College didn't work that way.

Truth: I didn't know how college worked at all.

I didn't know, for instance, that you had to have an academic advisor. I didn't know, for instance, that you had to take certain classes—that some were required and some were elective—in order to graduate. I simply thought you took classes that interested you and then at the tail end of the fourth year, they handed you a diploma and wished you luck. I didn't know, for instance, that you had to pick a major. On my first morning in the registration office, someone whisked me into an office where a very nice but harried woman jabbed at her computer keyboard and, in one arbitrary stroke, declared me a communications major. "You can change it later," she said. And I would change it, as it happened, to theatre arts.

Put another way, I didn't know the *language*. Nor did I know the lay of the land. I could no more navigate the academic landscape than I could the social landscape. One afternoon after class, I found myself at my desk poring over my humanities text, when Mark barreled through the door with a flyer in hand. "We've got to rush," he said. I sat in my seat blank-faced.

"You know—a fraternity."

"But I won't get in," I said.

Mark laughed. "Of course you'll get in."

"I have long hair, and besides—"

"My brother was a Sigma Nu. That makes me a legacy. Hang with me and you're in. Simple."

"I don't have that kind of money."

"It's cheap. It's nothing."

Fraternity. The word carried weight. It seemed elusive somehow, rare and unreachable. It was what other people joined. I was a boy from the scabland, all sticks and brush. My people wore their worst clothes to work, not their best. My people lost limbs and digits in on-the-job machinery. My people drove flatbed trucks rigged with arc welders. My people knew the scents of diesel, grease, and sage and relied upon them as constants in their worlds, the way they relied upon coffee or the quartered elk in the deepfreeze. My people didn't join fraternities. Fraternities were fancy, and my people didn't do fancy.

And yet I always had one foot in my tribe and one foot out, and the one foot in said stay the hell away from such uppityness. The one foot out, though, was curious, and after all, I had a head full of dreams.

First, some clarifications. My school was in the iron grip of Iron County, a hotbed of conservatism fueled almost wholly by the overwhelming Mormon presence, whose people dropped their wagon hitches there in the middle of the nineteenth century. (The Mountain Meadows Massacre occurred some thirty miles south of my college town, and that event is still something of an awkward if not haunting barb in that town's history).

Mormons don't do fraternities either, as one might guess. So our campus had at the time two fraternities (Sigma Nu and a local petitioning chapter, Delta Sigma Chi), and two local sororities (Phi Alpha Beta and Chi Sigma Upsilon). The die-hard Mormon kids (or Mo-Mos, as they were called) had their own fraternity and sorority, but I saw them as cheesy, soda-pop operations, and so did most students, even the more progressively minded Mormons. So it wasn't much of a Greek system. Of course each chapter's membership had a streak of Mormonism running through it, but it varied in degree from house to house and pledge class to pledge class. Also, only Sigma Nu and Phi Alpha Beta had official houses. Sigma Nu, the one Mark intended to rush, was populated with tall, tan guys with shiny watches, guys who bathed in cologne and sported golf memberships. Most of them came from money (by Utah standards) or at least looked the part. Phi Alpha Beta consisted of driven, business-minded women. They were beautiful and smart and clearly out of my reach. Chi Sigma Upsilon, like Phi Alpha Beta, was populated with smart, driven, and beautiful women as well, but they seemed more progressive. If Phi Alpha Betas wore Ann Taylor, the Chi Sigs wore Birkenstocks. Delta Sigma Chi, the local petitioning fraternity, was an anomaly. Their membership had a wider Mormon streak than Sigma Nu had, but they also had a small group of drinkers among them. Moreover, they didn't *look* like a fraternity. They came in all shapes and sizes. Tall, short, round, lean, freckled, tan, macho, straight, gay, brown, white.

Only two among them looked the fraternity type, and they were referred to as the "founding fathers." Puffed out chests, Guess jeans, and catalogue smiles.

If I attended a Sigma Nu event, I do not recall it. Fact is I felt entirely uncomfortable around all of them. What's more, I didn't want to continue in Mark's shadow. While I learned much from him, and would continue to learn much from him, I needed to retire my status as Mark's Roommate, and strike out under my own name. It was time to make some distinctions. So I opted to investigate the local fraternity, Delta Sigma Chi (which would later receive a charter as Sigma Chi).

My first rush event, which was held not at a house, but at a park, was a barbeque affair, and the Chi Sigma Upsilon sorority (or Chi Sigs), was there in full force. The weather was warm. The girls wore sundresses. Frisbees sailed through the air. Burgers smoked on the grill, and everyone was drinking soda or fruit punch.

At some point I got into a conversation with a beautiful girl named Nella. She wore a tie-dye shirt and Birkenstocks and a beaded necklace. Each of us had our paper plates loaded down with chips, potato salad, and fruit. I had a burger. She did not. And I made some query about her burgerless plate.

She laughed. "I'm a vegetarian."

"A who?"

"A vegetarian."

I just stared at her. My people ate meat with side-dishes of meat and more meat. "So you don't, like, eat burgers?"

"I don't eat meat."

"But you do on Thanksgiving and Christmas."

Her turn to offer a blank stare. "No. I don't eat meat."

"But sometimes, like occasionally."

"I. Don't. Eat. Meat."

"So you don't eat meat?"

"No."

"Weird."

"Why is that weird?"

"I don't know. Because everyone eats meat, I guess."

She laughed. "You're funny."

A moment of awkwardness passed between us and we turned to scan the crowd to see if we needed to be somewhere else. Then one of the Delta Sigma Chis joined us. He was kind in a disarming way. Soft spoken, yet confident. No airs. No bravado. No headiness. Nella turned to him and said, "Have you met Brandon?"

We shook hands. He was Founding Father Number 3, I would later learn. His name was Todd.

"Brandon's from Idaho," Nella said. "He's not a vegetarian."

I laughed uneasily. And soon, Todd had taken over the conversation and started telling anecdotes and a couple of stories, and then whatever he had said, and I now forget, but it reminded me of a similar story which I started to tell. But halfway through my telling, I was interrupted. At some point, I had said, "We *was* running down the street."

Potato salad nearly shot out of Nella's nose. "Did you just say, 'We *was* running'?"

I froze, my mouth locked. I tried to say something and my face and ears shot red.

"Oh, *come on*, Nell!" Todd said, laughing. "What is this, English class?" He then turned to me, clapped his hand on my shoulder, and said, "*Girls*, right? What are you gonna do?"

Todd steered me in another direction, where I was introduced to another group of guys. But as soon as I was done eating, I dropped my plate and fork in the trash and made the long and miserable trip back to my dorm room. I had been humiliated on two counts and felt lost and angry. Inside, the room was still. Outside, night was gathering and I could hear crickets beyond the window screen. I sat down at my desk, switched on my desk lamp, and stared at my small group of books on the shelf above my desk. I stared at them a good long while with my arms folded in front of me. My head kept replaying Nella's words over and over again, a monstrous, relentless loop of humiliation: *Did you just say we* was *running?* Then I did something positively dorky. I pulled two books down from my shelf—two that I had picked up at the campus bookstore. The first was Strunk and White's *The Elements of Style,* and the second was Fitzgerald's *The Great Gatsby.* And there beneath the lampglow of my small dorm room, a world away from home, I made, in my usual melodramatic way, some vows and no small promises that such an ambush, such a cultural misstep would never happen again. I would not, from that day forward, let the Idaho boy in me betray the man I wanted to become. So I cracked *The Elements of Style* (which was recommended, but not required, in my English 101 class) and flipped to the Introduction. "The reader," White writes, "will soon discover that these rules and principles are in the form of sharp commands," Sergeant Strunk, snapping orders to his platoon. "Do not join independent clauses with a comma." (Rule 5.) "Do not break sentences in two." (Rule 6.) "Use the active voice." (Rule 14.) It was clear, clean writing about how to write (and, I hoped, speak) cleanly and clearly. An hour passed. Then two. And I stayed with those pages. Rule 9 was of special use: "The number of the subject determines the number of the verb." I jotted down notes and underlined some passages. Memorized lines. Even tried a few exercises. What a geeky thing to do! And how liberating! I had the room and this book and my new promises all to myself. I was coming alive in my small world and I was learning its language.

Later I crawled into my twin bed and opened *The Great Gatsby.* Unlike EOS, this book was not for class. I bought it because I hadn't read it and because it seemed like one of those books that should have appeared on one of my crumpled receipts in my Metallica wallet but wasn't.

If I could simply turn off the filmic moments that swam from my memory in haunting detail—the crowd in the English building snickering at my mustardyness, the vegetarian flap, quickly followed by my grammatical implosion—I would be fine, I could concentrate on the book. But I couldn't turn them off. Over and over again, the embarrassments replayed in my mind. Slowly, though, as I eased into the pages of *The Great Gatsby*, I started to see a world consumed by class and quaked by even bigger collisions. Mark called me "Mate," not "old sport," but I began to see Mark through a Gatsbian lens, though I was no Nick Carroway.

The more I read, the more I ached to live elsewhere, somewhere east, in a place people knew. Some place like Boston or New Haven or Princeton. And the more I ached to be someone else. And soon a whine-a-thon rang in my head. Why couldn't I have been born into money? Why couldn't I have thought about college early on, or have been born into a family who would have thought about it on my behalf, long before I came into this world as another beating heart? Why couldn't I don fine clothes and enjoy the blithe thoughtlessness of a flush bank account and sit around a room drinking mint juleps on languorous afternoons spiked with desire and sex and all athrum to the song of the American Dream?

In other words, I was in the throes of self-pity and I was also beginning to love *The Great Gatsby* for all the wrong reasons. Sure, I could see the tack the book was taking toward an America hollowed out by greed and the cruelties of wicked men, but I also wanted the very things that were leading to their inevitable ruination. Mine were foolish dreams but I was young and foolish and high on possibilities and my dreams were haunted by a green light at the end of the dock, and the way to that green light, I thought, was through social climbing. One rung on that ladder was a fraternity. Ironically, it may have been *The Great Gatsby* alone, and its haunting pages of yellow cars and mint juleps and the seductive lull of jazz that convinced me I should take rush seriously. I wanted in some deep and unnamable way to be a part of the social order, which is another way of saying I was still trying to ascend some Dickensian wall.

The days that tumbled afterward hummed with electricity. It was the tail end of Rush Week, Fall Quarter, 1991, and I was hundreds of miles away from home walking around in some imponderable stupor. I might as well have been a million miles away from home, from small town Idaho. I might as well have landed on another planet. Outside, the earth was red and arid and slot canyons snaked off in every direction. Sandstone spires jutted skyward, the sky a wash of metallic blue. I found myself in a world of books, not of tools, trucks, or guns. I couldn't have been more strange to such a strange land. I was by turns thrilled and worried. I was thrilled to be on the green lawns of a university. Thrilled to sit in classes in ivied brick buildings. Thrilled beyond thrilled to see all the hot girls. Worried that I was out of place. Worried that I wasn't smart enough for my classes. Worried that the hot girls would never see me. Worried that I wouldn't be asked to pledge.

Turns out, my worries were justified on this latter point. It was Friday and bids, I knew, would be hand delivered that evening. After classes, I headed to my dorm room to study and while away the hours. Mark dropped in. He had already been given his bid to pledge Sigma Nu. He was going to a party at their house that evening. "What about you?" he asked, meaning had I been extended a bid yet.

"I don't think it's going to happen."

"It'll happen. They seem like good guys."

"Yeah."

"Listen, Brandon," he said. "Not to worry, mate. You'll get in." He refreshed his cologne, checked his teeth in the mirror and messed with his hair. "I'm meeting this Betty out on the quad to study. Nice fucking tits, mate. Perfect. I'm hoping to hit that shit."

"I'm sure you will."

It was difficult not to envy Mark and his playboy ways. Everything worked out for Mark. He had a near preternatural way of tapping into the social circuitry of any place he inhabited. Girls rang our phone for Mark, knocked on our door looking for him, orbited him in the student union—all in the first two weeks of school. It was uncanny. Meanwhile, I stood in the margins, which, in a sense, was the best thing I could have done. Mark was all confidence. I had very little. And so I became an observer. But the cruelest thing about observing, if you do it attentively and honestly, is that you begin to see the world in a different, less naïve way. Curtains are drawn back. The script and rules are revealed in sobering detail. Mark knew he would get his bid from Sigma Nu like he knew he would draw another breath. That was observable. And as the hours ticked by that evening, and as I paced my dorm room floor, reading the pages of *The Great Gatsby*, I was beginning to observe the gray reality that I wasn't cut out for the fraternity lifestyle, despite Mark's assurances. And as the hours ticked by, my attentions were torn between Fitzgerald's story and the case I was building in my head against the possibility of receiving a bid. There was a lot to add to the case, my grammatical trespass notwithstanding, and most of it, I think, stemmed from the Rush Interview Sheet, which looked something like this:

1. Please tell us a little about yourself. What are some of your favorite activities (i.e., golf, tennis, traveling)? What were your greatest accomplishments in high school? What other clubs do you belong to here at school (i.e., Presidential Ambassadors, student government, intramurals, church clubs, etc.)? Are you an athlete?
2. What do you expect to gain from Delta Sigma Chi if extended a bid? In turn, what do you expect to contribute to our fraternity?
3. Are you currently social with anyone in the sorority system? If so, please list their name(s) and the nature of your relationship.
4. Please list your high school GPA (be honest, please): ——.
5. Define brotherhood.

I remember panicking at the outset. I couldn't very well list playing guitar in a heavy metal band as an activity. So I wrote "music." I also wrote, "reading." I could, however, list my stint as student body vice president even though I knew it sounded more impressive than the "job" actually was. But I didn't belong to any clubs on campus, so there was a blank there. I recall feeling confident about the second question largely because I could bullshit a lot of it, and I was good at bullshitting (my nickname in high school was B.S., after all.). The third question was alarming, actually, and strange. But it was painful, too, because I could only recall the name of one sorority girl—Nella—and I wasn't about to put hers on the list. So that went blank too. Like an idiot, I answered the fourth question—the one about my high school grades—honestly. I scribbled down my C average fearing that fraternity guys could somehow access my high school transcripts and call me out. I felt easier about the last question because it was vague, and I could do vague. The more specific the questions got, the more I started to feel skewered. So the whole interview sheet was a mixed bag at best. Add the mixed interview to my long hair, screwball clothing, grammatical trespass, and God only knows what else, and it all amounted to a "Thanks, but no thanks."

Soon, it became obvious that I wouldn't be receiving a bid. It was nearly 10:00 p.m. and the scuttlebutt on our hallway was that most, if not all, of the bids had been delivered. I felt, on the one hand, gut-punched, but on the other, at ease. *Why does it matter? Who cares about their stupid club anyway?* I remember thinking. I tried to talk myself down from the precipice of disappointment by disparaging the whole notions of fraternities in general. I could paint them all one color and be done with it. Done with the worrying, the nonsense. I would just be me, and that would be enough.

Then a knock at the door. It was almost 11:00. I marked my page in *The Great Gatsby*, turned down my music, and answered the door. A tall, clean-cut, towheaded guy in a Delta Sigma Chi sweatshirt who looked absolutely German, stood before me with a wide grin and an envelope. "Congratulations, man," he said. "Here's your bid to pledge."

I said thanks and took the thick envelope, said goodbye, and sat on my bed in disbelief. Inside, it gave me the rundown. Time for my first meeting. What to bring. Where to go. All of it. I was thrilled and slightly nauseous. I read it again. And again. What I didn't know at the time, and could not have known, is that there was, in fact, a reason for the delay in receiving my bid. I didn't know, for instance, that the fraternity had been locked in a chapter meeting for hours hotly debating two prospective pledges: a guy who lived with his girlfriend (which the Mormon faction took to be sinister and wicked), and yours truly because of my long hair (which the Mormon faction singled out as it conveyed a "partier image"). In the end, however, both pledges in question were extended bids, however tentative they might have been. But I didn't know any of this at the time, and would only learn later, perhaps years later, the ways in which I had become something of a wedge issue in the chapter. But at the time, I was pleased and felt lucky. Then, before I turned to sleep, I slipped the bid in its envelope, and slipped the envelope in *The Great Gatsby* to mark the page, and turned off the light.

I was in.

Flaubert, Gustave. *Madame Bovary: Life in a Country Town*. Vol. 2 of *Norton Anthology of World Masterpieces*, 6th ed., edited by Maynard Mack, Bernard M. W. Knox, John C. McGalliard, P. M. Pasinetti, Howard E. Hugo, Patricia Meyer Spacks, Rene Wellek, Kenneth Douglas, and Sarah Lawall. New York: Norton, 1992.

As an only child who tended toward melodrama, I very often felt sorry for myself for any number of things. For a broken shoelace, a flat bike tire, a failed relationship—for having grown up in a blue-collar family in Idaho. You name it. When something went wrong, I was sure to go on a streak of self-loathing, especially if that something was genuinely grim.

Usually, when you least expect it, something genuinely grim comes your way. In the summer of 1995, the year I should have graduated from college had I not still been classified—by credits completed—as a freshman, I convinced five of my fraternity brothers to join me on a road trip to Soda Springs, Idaho. It would be a Great and Grand Idaho Odyssey. Incredibly, they agreed.

I had just purchased a 1987 Toyota Land Cruiser, a big wagony box of a rig, and had volunteered it for the trip. When I bought it, I got a temporary registration and bought insurance, but the plates were still the old California plates that came with it, and the temporary registration was only valid for a few more days. It was, to my thinking, close enough to be road worthy.

The drive north from Cedar City, Utah, to Soda Springs, Idaho, is around six or seven hours. All high mountain desert. A straight shot north that runs parallel to jagged peaks of the Wastach Front. But we had stops along the way. One, to pick up a guy in Provo where he had been doing fieldwork for the Division of Wildlife Resources. And another to stop in Salt Lake for a bite to eat and beers. Our weekend bender started there in a brewery in Salt Lake. We toasted the Great and Grand Idaho Odyssey, paid our tabs, and motored north, our heads buzzing with beery goodness.

Rewind one week, to the previous weekend. I am hiking through a mountain meadow in southern Utah with a couple of guys and a couple of girls, and we have all eaten some mushrooms, and have smoked a little pot, and feel contented that the world is blazing with meadow flowers and gnarled with bristlecone pines. It's one of a hundred such hikes I have taken and everything looks cartoonish and my friends look a like Muppets and all is swell in the world.

The next day, however, I wake in my bed with some serious itching down in my boxers. Like fiery itching. Like you-have-boned-a-vat-of-crabs-itching. So I am freaked out that all my years of rubber-less, careless sex have come home to roost in what looks like eight thousand itchy red spots all over my sex gear. Trouble there is, I had been seeing this really hot girl I had met at work, a girl who was icy and petite and hugely sarcastic and smart; a girl, in other words I wanted desperately because no one, so far as I could see, had gotten with her, had opened that door.

Her name was Kyle and she was from Downey, California, and was antisocial in a way that only made her seem cooler. She was no sorority girl, this one. She wore jeans and dock martens and thong underwear and I couldn't get enough of her. And for a long time, the feeling was mutual. We had become a couple, a thing, and she would spend the night at my house, or vice-versa, where we would tear it up beneath the sheets.

So when the itching arrived, I didn't know quite how to break it to her. I had been monogamous, so there seemed to me only one explanation. I had gotten the nasty disease from Kyle. When I summoned the nerve, I drove to her apartment, and stood before her with my hands busy in my pockets, doing the itchy dance in her living room. "Well?" I said. "Do you have it, too?"

She laughed at me. "That's what you get for hooking up with a skank."

"I haven't done shit! That's why I'm here!" And after more itchy-dancing, I lay on her couch scratching like a dog plagued by the wrath of fleas.

All the while she just laughed at me. This was typical Kyle. No sympathy. No bullshit.

That was Sunday afternoon.

On Monday, I paid a visit to the campus health clinic, where at the front desk, I whispered, "venereal disease," meaning that's what I thought I had.

Inside the examination room, I stood before the doc with my pants down while he took his time looking at each red spot. Finally, he scribbled on the clipboard, clicked his pen, and said, "Spider bites."

"Spider bites?"

He stood at the skink washing his hands. "Have you been hiking lately?"

As a matter of fact I had, and my mind circled back to the mushroomy meadow of glory and the tall grasses I had tramped through.

Because I am allergic to penicillin, he gave me a subscription of erythromycin, which, as it turns out, worked like a charm.

I had lucked out on the VD front, and as long as I had that little bottle of pills, I was good. When I told Kyle the news, she just laughed again, and then said, "Come here," and kissed me.

So among the many necessities that I had to pack for the Great and Grand Idaho Odyssey, my itchy meds ranked number one.

We reached Soda Springs late in the afternoon after a quick stop at an ice cave where, in its chilly darkness, a couple of our cohort sparked up a joint and got stoned and giggled as they crabbed their way over slick dark rocks.

What ensued afterward—when we hit town—was a typical frat-boy bar crawl. Begin at the pizza place and order four pitchers of beer for the five of you. When the twelve-year old server asks, on your way out, "Are you guys okay to drive?" Your response will be to belch and hoot and holler incoherencies meaning, "Shit, yeah! We couldn't be better!"

In all there are four bars in Soda Springs. Three downtown. One on the outskirts by the golf course. You plan to hit them all. But by bar number three, things are starting to get boozy, a little unhinged. One fellow fraternity brother falls backward off his barstool and is later found vomiting in the bathroom. The rest of us are doing "Welcome to the Jungle" on the karaoke stage, but are quickly booted for banging the microphones on the stage railing.

Three down and one to go. It's nearing midnight as we stagger through the street and pile into the Land Cruiser. Does it occur to us that we shouldn't be driving? That we could be killed, or kill someone else? That maybe three bars is good enough and we should call it a night? That my grandmother's house (which is where we are staying) is one block away and that you could be home in five minutes on foot?

Not on your life.

What happened next goes something like this. I aim the Land Cruiser due west, toward the golf course, and am doing my best to stay between the lines. But when the car in my rear view speeds up to the point that our bumpers nearly kiss, and then when he hits those lights—the blues and the reds—we freak. "Pull over, Schrand." Someone says. "Get him some gum," someone else says.

But we all know. Oh, we know. We are *so* fucked.

Here's what we did *not* have going for us:

1. Two of us had weed on their persons. (I was not one of them).

2. One had a loaded 9 mm, having brought it with him from his fieldwork (where you do occasionally need a sidearm).
3. Expired plates.
4. No seat belts (a drunken move on our part because we typically wore them).
5. And one of us flashed a fake ID.

After I failed the roadside sobriety test, I was cuffed. Drunk, dumb, and desperate, I cited "benefit of clergy," a seventeenth-century legal loophole Ben Johnson had once invoked when facing murder charges. Because he could read scripture in Latin, the reasoning went, he was above the law and therefore exonerated on that count. That I couldn't cite *any* scripture in Latin or otherwise, didn't diminish my boozy hopes of the loophole's potential. The arresting officers were unimpressed, and my friends kept begging me to stay quiet.

In the end, they let two of us go, and arrested the other three of us. Perhaps what we *did* have going for us was that I knew the arresting officer fairly well. His wife had worked in our café when I was in high school and, awesomely enough, my parents and I went to the zz Top concert (the Afterburner Tour) with him and his wife in the Pocatello Mini-Dome. And that may be why all of us didn't share the pot charges, why the registration offense was dropped, along with the seatbelt infractions. Why, in the end, I was arrested on DUI charges and that was trouble enough.

That was Saturday night.

Sunday morning was a gray hell of hangover misery. My grandmother bailed us out, and we spent the rest of the day trying to get my Land Cruiser out of impound. But because it is sagebrush country, the guy who runs the impound yard likes to go fishing on Sundays, and so we would just have to wait until Monday to get it out. Meanwhile my itching had flared to an atomic fury, and my medication was in the Land Cruiser.

So I called the police station several times, "I need my medication," I said. "And I need it right now."

"I'm sorry but the arresting officer is off duty, and won't be able to look into this situation until this evening."

"What part of I-Need-My-Medication-Right-Now do you not understand?"

"I *am* sorry."

I slam the phone down.

I called again. Then once more, each time, my anger—which was peaking in direct proportion to the inflammation of the red-hot spider bites in my shorts—less and less reserved. "Listen: You CAN NOT keep my medication from me, do you understand?"

"I told you I was sorry . . ."

"HOW ABOUT THIS: When I fucking SUE your ass, then you will know what sorry means! HOW ABOUT THAT? *HUH?* Do you want to be the one to tell the judge why you withheld my medication? Do you? Or should it be someone else? Because someone is accountable here. *I-want-my-medication-right-fucking-now.*"

I slam down the phone again, and my friends who are enduring their own miseries are laughing at my temper tantrum but are also issuing caution: "You better be careful of what you say, Schrand."

"I can't take it any longer!" I shout.

"If you'd stop fucking skanky hookers, your dick wouldn't itch."

More laughter. I bat my hand at them.

At some point, mid-afternoon, they release my car from impound, I take my pills, and we make a long and quiet journey home.

My punishment rightly included a fine of a few hundred dollars, license suspension, SR-22 (high risk) insurance, alcohol counseling, and two days behind the iron clang of county bars. I was scheduled to report to jail two weeks later.

There was no crash, no injuries, no blinding race to the hospital, but that night remains a blot in my memory, and I cringe when I think of the what-ifs and what-could-have-beens. An on-

coming car, a sudden flood of headlights, a pedestrian, or a cyclist cartwheeling over the hood of my vehicle. The reality was
stark enough.

When I reported to the courthouse on the first morning of my
incarceration, I had one book with me, a jumbo literary anthology the size of a Buick from my World Literature course. It's the
kind you see pale and emaciated English majors lugging around
the student union, or reading in dark coffee shops that play
Morrissey. It contained, among other fine reads, selections from
Dostoevsky, which I planned to read because I tended toward
melodrama, and Flaubert's *Madam Bovary*, which I knew was being assigned for a class I was taking in the fall. The anthology,
which I still own, is flagged here and there with sticky notes and
contains two items of interest. (1) A photocopy of a map that
reads "Africa 1914" (no idea why that is in there); and (2) a
sparkly Hunter S. Thompson *Fear and Loathing in Las Vegas* book-
mark folded into the *Madame Bovary* section. My insipid marginalia (which I can't recall whether I wrote in jail or afterward
(would they have allowed me a pen??)) includes clunkers like
"Hot Sex Scene" and "Poignant religious commentary."

For whatever reason, my parents sprang for a lawyer, which
was weird because it was a non-issue: I was drunk. I had been
driving. I got caught. Guilty on all counts. But they insisted. "Just
in case," they said. But on that morning, my lawyer—a thin, dar-
ty-eyed man, likely fresh out of law school—met me at the jail
to help with last minute details.

As we walked toward the check-in area that I remember as a
counter manned by a police officer, and an iron door that
buzzed when you walked through it, I stopped and said, "Do
you think I can take this book in with me?"

"Uh," he said, looking at it quickly. "What is it?"

"It's an anthology," I said, and then added, "For a class. In
the fall."

He shrugged, took a sip of coffee from a paper cup, and asked
the man behind the counter if I could take it in.

"What is it?"

"It's his anthropology book."

"Anthropology?"

"For school," my lawyer said.

"Actually, it's an *anthology* . . ." I corrected.

They both looked at me, irritated.

"Whatever," the officer said, meaning yes.

My bed was a thin rubber mat with a transparent sheet and a pillow no thicker than a sock. I wore an orange jumpsuit and brown rubber sandals. The toilet was stainless steel with a drinking fountain attached to its back, suggesting, somehow, that you were drinking toilet water, and so after a cursory glance at the plumbing, I felt more, not less, uneasy. The shower was also stainless steel and cylindrical so that if felt like you were standing inside a soda can or the barrel of a gun. I showered only once but did not drink from the fountain/toilet contraption. Instead, I read Flaubert. And I read the book with a strange hunger. I read nonstop for two days. I read as a way to beat back the iron, to color the gray, and to obliterate the cruel quiet of incarceration. I wanted again to tumble headlong into that world of daydreams, to find my way back to a simpler place. But most of all I wanted to absolve myself. Read the story, pass the class, and none of this ever happened.

Hacker, Diane. *The Bedford Handbook for Writers.*
3rd ed. Boston: Bedford Books of St. Martin's
Press, 1991.

If I felt out of place on campus, in my own skin, in social
settings, or even in my own dorm room, I found comfort
in my English 101 composition class. It is a class I will not
soon forget. Our instructor was Don Scanlan, and he also
happened to be the editor of the campus newspaper, *The
Thunderbird* (named for our mascot). Don was in his early
forties, single, and amusing. He dressed well, possessed a
razor wit, but was something of a mystery. He had, I knew,
graduated from Brigham Young University, but his irrev-
erence in the classroom was not only delightful, but it
seemed to belie what I could only assume was his Mormon
background. He had something of a flamboyant streak
that was tempered, too, by a kind of toughness you see in
editors on television, the ones who bark from their offices,
slam phones, and who smoke too much. He was great.

I liked the class, too, because there was a girl named
Anne who was boner-in-your-pants hot. She sat on the front
row and wrecked me with her long dark hair, tan legs that
went on forever, and her sass. I think Don liked her too,
because they always bantered back and forth, with his wit
out-pointing her sass almost always, and with her occasional knockout comment. I was smitten. And, like me,
she lived in the dorms. And like everyone else on campus,
she simply knew me as Mark's Roommate. I never missed
my composition class that I can recall, because I thought
Don rocked, but mostly because I didn't want to miss out

on Anne's legs and how they would destroy me for one hour a day, three times a week.

Other things I recall about that class. It was taught in the music building, ground level, so its floor-to-ceiling windows faced the quad. When I wasn't daydreaming about how to get between Anne's long legs, I could simply gaze into the green quad and daydream about whatever floated into my mind: my fraternity, partying, the future, the books I might one day read.

And although Diana Hacker's text *The Bedford Handbook for Writers* didn't swim its way into my daydream of books I might one day read or appear on my receipt lists as a book one should have read while at college, I do recall taking it seriously in the same way I took Strunk and White's *Elements of Style*. Don had selected it, and not EOS, he said, because we had to write a research paper, and EOS didn't teach you that, what with all the MLA formatting and citations. He could have assigned both, but he was trying to save us some money, he said with a wink.

Honestly, I don't remember whether we ever wrote a research paper or not. But I do recall clearly one paper in particular. It was a "personal essay" assignment that drew upon some memory or memories that were significant to us—the very kind of essay I would use, years later, to teach my own college freshman. He gave us the weekend, and on Monday we filed into our classroom where he had arranged the desks in a great circle. We were to read our essays aloud, and for whatever reason, the long-haired kid from the scrub-brush of Idaho was not the first to go, but the last.

A couple of things. First, my essay was titled something like "White Pants, a Guy Named Clay, and Glass-Bottomed Shoes," and centered on what I then took to be the "worst night of my life." Second, my essay was handwritten. Blue ball point pen on notebook paper. It was maybe four pages long and instead of stapling the leaves together, I tied them with a piece of gold thread, thinking, you know, that it was much *fancier* that way. I didn't type the essay because (1) I never learned how to type, and (2) I was in college on the cutting edge of computers, and although my small university had a computer lab, the dot matrix printers were almost too cumbersome to deal with, so I took pen to paper, which, shockingly, Don was cool with (another reason why, in my estimation, he rocked).

It was my background in theater, I think, that fueled my aching desire to perform, to read aloud, and I saw my chance to read my essay, however bad, as such a chance. Moreover, our circular seating arrangement put me across from Anne and her long legs, which increased the stakes considerably for my reading. (My thinking here, of course, was that a stellar essay would lead to sex with Anne). Student after student read and I would compare each essay to mine. Finally, at a few minutes before the bell, it was my turn. As I read, my pulse turned electric. If my ears shot red, and they likely did, I don't recall. I just remember reading my essay and at the end, Don's response. He looked around the class and said, "Well—would anyone like to take their essays home and rewrite them?" And everyone agreed. "Mr. Schrand," he said. "You can leave yours."

I was embarrassed. I was stunned. And I was hoping that Anne was sexually aroused. On the way out of the classroom, she threw me a welcome dish of sass: "Well, aren't *you* a brown-noser." She laughed.

"How was that brown-nosing?"

"You are *such* a suck-up, Brandon Schrand."

Anne: always using the full name.

"Suck up? What about *you?*"

Like all flirtatious volleying, our banter went back and forth like this as we crossed the quad back to Juniper Hall. The late-afternoon autumn desert sun was angled slightly to the west. Shadows grew longer, deeper. The grass was green. The skies were clear and I felt like I was living, breathing, thinking for the first time in my life. The essay was a small success, but it was my first moment of validation in college, the first time I felt like I could really cut it in a place where ivy clung to brick, where girls walked the quad in heart-stopping skirts, and where professors scuttled around with their noses in books. What's more is that I caught Anne's attention, if only fleetingly.

In the dorm lobby, Anne and I parted ways. She took the stairs to the girls' wing, and I took the stairs to the boys' wing. It occurs to me now that I should write the women's wing and the men's wing, but I don't think we were women or men. I think we were unabashedly boys and girls thrust into the world of men and women, and just as I had some notion that the creek bottom I used to haunt would one day vanish, so too did we know, deep in our blood, that our lives as we had come to know them on the bright green grasses of the quad would also vanish. From the top of the stairs, Anne called out to me. "Take care, Brandon Schrand," she said, and then added, "Suck up," for good measure. And I watched her slip into her hallway.

Back in C-219, Mark was napping. He was a nap enthusiast, which I respected from a distance. So I slid into my chair at my desk and opened Diana Hacker's book. I had some exercises due, and now that I had drawn so much attention to myself in Don's class, I felt as if there were some new expectations in place.

I had completed a few short exercises—on fixing dangling modifiers, or parallel structures, or some other clue into the mystery of our written tongue—when Mark's alarm sounded and he sprung from his bed. "Cocktail, mate?"

"Sure."

From our mini-fridge, Mark exhumed a quart of orange juice and a pint of vodka and mixed two generous drinks in plastic cups. And before we toasted, he did something that was as repulsive as it was shocking but that was also what I would learn to be signature-Mark. He reached down the front of his pants, scratched around his balls, and then sprinkled a dash of pubes into his cocktail. "Bottom's up!" He was cracking up, drunk on his own hilarity.

"That's the most fucked up thing I've ever seen, man."

"What?"

I shook my head and took a long pull off the screwdriver.

The Bedford Handbook for Writers was the book I took most frequently to my pledge class study hall, which was held on the third floor of the library. The library was an ugly thing, an unfortunate architectural blunder of the 1960s. It was square, more or less, and looked like a giant lid to a bottle of engine coolant. Strangely, it had more floors underground than it did above ground, and as a partial consequence of this subterranean design, it boasted not a single window in its aboveground floors. It was a design that felt remotely cruel, like a punishment, and one that smacked of bibliophilic discipline. God forbid a student's gaze might disconnect from the book at hand and find itself pondering the quad outside and the daydreams it held.

That I was obligated to log time there as part of my duties in the Delta Pledge Class of Delta Sigma Chi only compounded, in my mind, the suffocating feeling the library imparted.

In all, there were twelve of us in the pledge class. A cool dozen. Local guys made up a majority of the group, which meant that most of them were of the Mormon variety. But each of them varied in his degree of faith, ranging from the devout kind who wouldn't say shit if his mouth was filled with it, to the kind who was only Mormon on paper—like me. One guy was from California. Another from Colorado. One from Nevada. Two—including me—from Idaho. And the rest who weren't local were from points around Utah. At the center of our cohort was Daniel, the younger brother of Todd, founding member No. 3, the guy who rescued me from my grammatical trip-up with Nella. Daniel, or Dan, could move a room, as they say. To say he was charismatic would be an understatement. Bespectacled, he was well-dressed, confident, winningly sarcastic, and smart. He was the kind of person who just looked smart, whose eyes revealed the serious machinations of a brain in high gear. His slightly babyish features suggested innocence and mischievousness in equal doses. As a non-Mormon in a Mormon stronghold, Dan knew well the heights one had to reach if he hoped to win favor in his world. And win favor he did. Wildly popular (and in some circles despised, meaning envied), Dan had distinguished himself in high school as a champion debater.

We became tight right away.

So it goes without saying that he was president of the Delta Pledge Class. He must have saw something in me too, because one night during study hall when we were hashing out pledge class elections, he kept urging me to step up for vice president, which I declined (and would regret the second I did). I took a lower position and the fact that I can no longer recall what it was speaks to its gravity (or lack thereof) in the small political sphere that made up our group.

A typical pledge night looked like this:

1. **Flagpole check-in at 6:00 p.m.** We met at the main flagpole on campus where we had to recite the pledge of allegiance and weekly drills. Because we were petitioning the national fraternity, Sigma Chi, much of what we had to recite was its codes and credos, but we also had to memorize the Greek alphabet and our local chapter's list of the twenty-six original founding fathers (and their PINs). At the end, the active brothers would take turns extolling little nuggets of what they took to be wisdom. They would also reiterate the importance of our appearance. Pledge pins should be worn with pride on the left breast of a *collared* shirt (much heated internal debate centered on whether or not polo shirts were too casual for pledge pins). A pledge must carry his *Norman Shield*—the official handbook to the Sigma Chi fraternity—with him at all times and collect signatures from active members only after interviewing them. Some signatures were easier to collect than others. Some active brothers would swell with pride as a pack of eager-beaver pledges swarmed them. Others—the more aloof of the group—thought it was cooler to be under the radar, and their signatures were prizes to be won. At the end of flagpole exercises, we would compare signatures.

2. **Study Hall at 7:00 p.m.** It was customary to march single file from the flagpole exercises directly to study hall, where we were given the first ten minutes to conduct official pledge class business. Typically, the active brother who presided over the study halls was our magister, or pledge marshal, Zack Petersen. Zack was an anomaly. A Southern California boy recruited to our school on a football scholarship (he was an offensive lineman and for damn good reason), Zack defied as many stereotypes as he typified. He was built like a meat locker and had a way of using his quiet, near silent demeanor as a weapon. But he was no bonehead in a bonehead major. On the contrary. Zack maintained a 4.0 average and majored in biology and secondary education. So his bulk at the head of the study hall table made for a decidedly quiet and productive session, and through it all, I would read my humanities text and the *Bedford Handbook for Writers*.

3. **Free Time at 9:00 p.m.** After two hours of monkish silence in serious study, we were antsy for the night and its elusive promise of sex, and so we were released until the next flagpole check-in, which was at 5:00 a.m. Because ours was a dry chapter on a dry campus, it followed that our pledge was also a dry pledge. So our nightly escapades didn't involve beer bongs and smoking spliffs and playing quarters (though all of that would come later); rather, it involved pranks (dreamed up by Dan primarily and amended by the rest of us), and those pranks were aimed at the sororities. Panty raids, while childish, cliché, and ultimately self-defeating, were the holy grail of Greek system pranks, at least in our young, sex-addled minds.

On an autumnal Monday evening that I recall for the wood smoke that hung in the air, the yellow-bellied harvest moon above, and the skiff of maple leaves damp on the ground, Dan had convinced Zack to let us out of our pledge meeting early to run such a prank on the Beta house. Like most Greek systems, all of our meetings were held on Monday evenings, which meant, in this case, that the Beta house would be empty for about two hours (they held their meetings on campus, as their living room was too small for all of them). Dan had revealed the details of our plan to Zack, who, in turn revealed them to his roommate, James—another SoCal offensive lineman 4.0 wonderboy—who in turn revealed the plan to Kevin, another active brother, who then revealed the plan to Heather, his current girlfriend and current president of the Beta house, who, in turn brokered the following deal: the kitchen window would be unlocked and she would guarantee that the house would be empty only if the Delta Pledge Class agreed *not* to touch the underwear of the Beta's executive council (which meant hers, and three others'). All other dressers and closets were fair game. Heather delivered these terms to Kevin, who told James, who delivered them to Zack, who delivered them to Dan, who delivered them to us. "You guys got it?" Dan asked pressingly at the end of our abbreviated pledge meeting. "We leave Heather's, Allison's, and Katrina's shit alone. Period."

We all nodded and tried, with no success, to stem the spasmodic bursts of laughter, the giddiness, the head-rush high and the penis-pulsing anticipation of fingering the silky things that touched the pinkest, most secret, sacred, fabled, dreamed-about, masturbated-to, parts of the hottest girls on campus. My god, think of our delight! My god, think of how we were such boys! Such wondrous boys! Could there be a more thrilling time in a boy's life than to stand on the precipice of the secret world of girls and peer in?

The Beta house was a large Victorian structure that gushed with pinks and mauves and great swagging valences and heavy curtains and floral carpeting and high-backed Victorian furniture. It had a great yard shaded by sky-reaching maples and was blanketed with October's leaves.

It must have been a sight too conspicuous to give it much

mind. Twelve snickering guys and their backpacks and flash-lights and dark clothing darting across campus in a single-mind-ed blitzkrieg quest for panties. Dan broke the group into teams: Recon and lookouts for both forward and rear installments. The rest of us gathered below the kitchen window. "Schrand's the scrawny one," Dan said. "He'll wiggle through the window and unlock the door. My heart knocked around and my ears thrummed red as I was given a leg up to the window. Once I poked my head through, I give a quick look around. Empty and dark. I scraped my stomach across the window jam and splayed my hands out in front of me until they hit the floor, and my legs followed. As planned, I unlocked the backdoor and signaled for the guys. Dan was the first one through. "Nice job, Schrand."

"Why didn't they just leave the back door unlocked?" I asked rubbing my sore stomach.

Dan snickered. "Isn't this great?"

Once in the living room, Dan—who had been in the Beta house even as a high school kid when he was hanging out with Todd—broke us once again into teams. Four guys, top floor; four guys, main floor. "Oh, and one more thing," Dan said. "No one leaves until all of Heather's, Allison's, and Katrina's draw-ers are cleaned out."

"But, that wasn't the deal," someone said.

I looked at Dan. He cracked up and said, "What deal?"

We moved from room to room, opening drawers and unleash-ing secrets. We filled our backpacks with bras and thongs and G-strings, giggling wildly over this one and that, ogling others that had teasers printed on them like "kiss me" and "boy toy" and so on. Some articles of underwear were, to our profound disappointment, ordinary and sackish—like something you might transport potatoes in; something an elderly woman in a fastidious Lutheran cooking club would wear. And what's a panty raid without at least one clown putting a pair on his head? So we did that too.

Soon it was called off. Our time was running out. "Let's split,"

Dan announced, and we filed out the back door, our backpacks stuffed and our horny imaginations sated.

Dan's was one of several getaway cars—a red Chevy Berretta GT—and it was his that I made a dash for. While several of us loaded in, Dan tied one of Katrina's bras to his radio antennae. As a double-D, it was a prize, a flag of victory, a battle cry. Dan jumped in, pleased with himself. He fired up the car, buckled his seatbelt and then looked at me, puzzled. "Seat belt."

"Huh?"

"Don't they have seat belts in Idaho?"

"Oh," I said, and fumbled to click it.

He laughed. "Jackass."

We had seat belts in Idaho, but no one wore them. My parents would mention it from time to time, but that was about it. Like my vegetarian snafu or the grammar bungle, this too was a moment that left me vulnerable and feeling behind the curve.

As it turned out, the timing couldn't have been better. As we burned down the street with a double-bazooka bra streaming from the antennae, we caught sight of the Betas walking from campus back to their house, and as we did, Dan started honking and waving another bra like a lasso out his window. We whooped and hollered and waved. They stood curbside all agawk and started to shout and pump their fists in the air.

If I was worried that none of these women would pay attention to me, I didn't need to worry any longer. I was in the middle of it, for better or worse.

As the girls raced to their house to assess damages, we raced to the quad and student center where we flung the underthings into the trees like Christmas ornaments. Then we posted a dozen flyers that read:

Scantily Clad Trees

Brought to You by the Sisters of Phi Alpha Beta

In a matter of twenty minutes Zack learned from Dan what had happened, that the deal was off. Zack then told James, who told Kevin, who called to tell Heather, who had already discovered for herself the breach. And in this way, we had become legendary in the eyes of our chapter and notorious with the women of the Beta house. We couldn't have been more pleased with ourselves.

We were boys and we were men humming with sexual energy. If emptying drawer upon drawer of red, pink, green, white, and blue underwear was thrilling for the non-virgins among us, it must have been cream-your-sheets orgasmic for the Mormon lads who were mission bound at the end of the fall term.

When Dan dropped me off at Juniper Hall that night, we shook hands. "Good times, Schrand," he said. I nodded and laughed, got out, and he drove off.

Inside, the dorm was quiet. But when I unlocked my dorm room door, I heard hushes and laughter and it was dark.

"Hey Mate," Mark called through the dark. Someone was with him.

"Sorry."

"No. You're fine. There's a beer in the fridge if you want one." And then: "Have you met Anne?"

And through the inky blue light came her voice: "Hi Brandon Schrand."

"Hey." My stomach crashed. I dropped my backpack on the bed, clicked on my lamp. "Give me just a sec, and I'll bail." My legs felt like rubber. Directly at my back lay Anne and those golden legs beneath the sheets, and she was naked, of course, because the soundtrack from *For Yours Eyes Only* murmured in the background.

"You can stay, Brandon. It's your room, too." Mark, I could tell was being sincere.

"No. It's cool. I just need my book." I unzipped my backpack and in the bottom was the *Bedford Handbook for Writers* tangled in an overlooked pair underwear. I pulled the book out, switched out the light, and started for the door.

"Goodnight, suck-up," Anne crooned through the darkness.

"Yeah," I said, and shut the door.

While Mark and Anne had what I imagined to be crazy, break-

Hacker, *Bedford Handbook for Writers* 67

the-bed, contortionist sex, I sat on a ratty dorm couch and thumbed through the Hacker guide for all of three minutes. On the other side of the lobby sat four caffeinated misfits playing D&D.

Soon I drifted off to sleep, and by the time I slipped into the dorm room the next morning, Anne was gone.

Hemingway, Ernest. *The Old Man and the Sea*. New York: Macmillan, 1980.

———. *The Sun Also Rises*. New York: Macmillan, 1987.

In high school (and later in college), I suffered from the disease of assignments. Once a book was *assigned*, I lost interest. But the books I discovered on my own—the *Mad Scientists' Club* or *The Great Gatsby* for instance—were just that: discoveries, not requirements. Very few assigned books became favorites during high school, but there were some to be sure: *Fahrenheit 451*, *Lord of the Flies*, and *To Kill a Mockingbird* were books that I accepted, if reluctantly, into my discretionary confidence. Others, though, I rejected flat-out. *Great Expectations*, *Les Miserable*, and the *Grapes of Wrath* amounted to a few thousand pages of time-suck, as far as I could tell. I couldn't be bothered. You are what you read—or so I thought—and I didn't want to be any of the characters in any of those books, thank you very much.

And so it was with Ernest Hemingway's epic tale, *The Old Man and the Sea*. It was assigned in my ninth-grade English class, and I recall meeting it with heady amounts of derision. I could not have cared less about some old dude in a stupid boat and a dumb fish and a little kid and the sharks and blah, blah, blah. It was, to my thinking, a complete waste of time.

It didn't help that we weren't actually *reading* the book, but rather listening to it on a cassette recorder in class. One day during our stint with Hemingway, we had a substitute teacher who, through no fault of her own (other than she was a sub and we were pimply blowhards), became our singular target. Shortly before we turned to the story on tape—and while the sub wasn't looking—my friend had absconded with the cassette player's AC cord. She inquired of its whereabouts, detecting, no doubt, some shenanigans afoot. "It doesn't need a cord," someone said. "Yeah," I seconded. "It's solar-powered." Everyone laughed. Everyone, that is, except for the sub, who stood before us with folded arms and flaring eyes. Meanwhile, as this poor woman rifled through cupboards for the cord, the captain of the wrestling team and all-around-cowboy, dropped a pinch of chewing tobacco in her coffee. It was a cruel trick, but we were rebelling in that unthinking and self-absorbed way that pubescent show-offs do, and any distractions that staved off old man Santiago and his fish were all to the good.

If we were punished for our antics, I don't recall the specifics. What I do recall, though, was that every afternoon afterward, while heat poured in through the old clanking radiators of our classroom and while snow billowed outside, our English teacher would stop the tape just before the bell, and I would wake from an unremembered dream to find my desk pooled with drool.

In college, however, I met up with Hemingway again, but on my own terms. And it could be said that I met up with him at the best of times and at the worst of times. I was in college, but I wasn't *in* college. Consider my transcripts from that term:

ARLE-101	COLLEGE ORIENTATION	F
ARLE-201	CONVOCATION	F
ENGL-206	CREATIVE WRITING	F
ENGL-251	INTRO TO POETRY	F
ENGL-492	PLAYWRITING	UW
	CURRENT GPA	0.00
	CUMULATIVE GPA	1.795

What is to account for the triple zero GPA? It's not like I was enrolled in o-chem or trig or Latin. Seriously, what is to account for failing college orientation? If the F-bomb in that class didn't symbolize my stumbling attempts to acclimate to a new order, then I don't know what would. This lineup would be a dream schedule for any wannabe writer, and yet I couldn't be bothered with the demands of great classes or the professors who taught them. Intro to Poetry was my favorite class, and I raved about the professor to my friends. A former Utah poet laureate, David Lee was, to me, a silver-haired rock star who made poetry cool, urgent, and necessary. Each lecture blew me away. Each lecture made me want to be a writer, made me go home and scribble down a poem and bring it to his office hoping to win sweeping praise. He would read it and issue limited praise and tell me to read Roethke, Milton, Hugo. So I was a dedicated student for all of four weeks, and then I'd vanish. It was the beginning of an old and worn-out pattern.

So, really, what was to account for this total failure, this flunky pattern? For one thing, I had been initiated into my fraternity, and while Mormons outnumbered other faiths and nonbelievers 7 to 1, there was a group I had fallen in with who liked to drink and who liked to smoke a little pot and drop acid and eat mushrooms. It was the early nineties, and southern Utah attracted a small countercultural group of tie-dye liberals who were enamored with its red-rock canyons and hiking. The guys who smoked pot in Soda Springs were, by and large, roughnecks. Big-truck construction workers and crowbar tough, they lived in trailer houses at the edges of town. Long hair and Bud Light. No frills. But the crowd I met in college was altogether different. They had money (relatively speaking), for one thing. And they were bookishly smart. And they were, well, in college, and they earned good grades and cared about larger, worldly things, like the environment, for instance. So when they asked me to smoke a bowl with them, not only was I persuaded because I admired them, wanted to dress like them, and wanted to be like them (money and all), but also because the mere weedy scent of pot smoke smelled like my childhood, like West Richland, and I couldn't help but feel at home in this kind of embrace.

And it was an embrace, as all druggie inductions are. There is a weird familial vibe to it all, and though it's a false vibe, it's convincing, lulling even, and before you know it, you're the one throttling up the bong and it's your lungs burning with the intake of smoke, and two hours later, your eyes are like two perforated slits in a pan of dough, and you have been laughing at absolutely nothing and everything, and the next day you sleep in, blow off classes, chuckle, and call the previous night one of the best ever.

My life had become an entire string of best nights (and days) ever. I was no longer just Mark's roommate. *I* was emerging. Or some version of me. This version blew off all classes so he could hike the red-rock mountains, alcoves, and slot canyons. How many afternoons, really, did I spend with my fraternity brothers on some trailhead with our hiking gear and a bag of weed? There isn't anything quite like standing in a sandstone alcove the size of a theater when you are stoned. The human scale goes out of whack and for the first time—either because of the weed or just because you are given to think about such things—you realize just how diminished you are in this landscape. You realize the scale of things, and that you will die. Your neck tires because you are forever looking up toward the dizzying sandstone spires, sheer walls of rock that thrust straight up for a thousand feet or more. You put your face against these walls time and time again as if you are listening but for what you cannot say. And when the snow melts, you watch the water fall in sheets, cascading toward earth and into the streams and arroyos that swell with runoff. In the battle of responsibility, between attending your business class or getting stoned in a box canyon, you always choose the latter. Hence the grades. Hence all the loose ends. Hence the wheels coming off. Hence the crashing joy of trying, and failing, to become a man.

This version of me got lucky in the chaos, though. One afternoon when Mark was gone, a knock came at my door. It was Anne. Tall and brunette and tan and smart and confident and sultry, and oh my god.

"Hi Brandon Schrand."

"Mark's gone," I said, sharper than I had intended.

"Oh," she said. "He said I could borrow his Bob Marley tape . . . ?"

I nodded and waved her in and scanned through his stacks of tapes while my heart fired like a canon in my chest. She was looking around. T-shirt and cutoff jeans. My hand was shaking as I fingered through his music collection, and I kept quiet at first, fearful that a warble in my voice would betray my desire. Then she sat on my bed.

"If you can't find it, it's not a big deal."

"It's . . ."

"So how *are* you, Brandon Schrand? We never *talk*, you know?" She crossed her legs and grabbed *The Great Gatsby*, which was on my pillow. And before I could say anything, she said, "So this is what a suck-up reads?" She laughed.

I turned and faced her. I made some teasing jab back, and she swatted my thigh with the book and looked at me, or into me. Or at me. It was difficult to read. Like any hormonal young man with a mind crazed with sex or its possibility, I was trying desperately to read the cues, the electric and kinetic waves that seemed (at least to me) to arc between us, but despite what I felt, what I could smell (Jesus, can you really smell mutual attraction?), my mind vacillated wildly between extreme verdicts: "It's so fucking on," and "You are an idiot, Schrand, she is here for Mark." All the while my mouth is speaking and of what I have no idea. I was on autopilot. Moments later, though, Anne had stretched out face down on my bed. It's a gutsy move and I am unclear as to what track of banter led to or allowed for such a move because it must be made under the guise of nonchalance lest the moment be ruined. And yet there was nothing casual about this girl lying on my bed. Then either I offered, or she asked—I can't remember which—but before I knew it, I was rubbing her back and her shoulders. Just like that. The old college cliché! Everyone knows that backrubs, when well administered (and even if not well administered), lead to sex. That backrubs constitute the gateway into the promised land. And there I was! Straddling her across the small of her back wondering if she could feel me grow hard in my pants. Fearful that she could feel it. Hopeful that she could feel it. Freaked beyond freaked that it was even happening. Still, even still, I couldn't be sure. Was I misreading the situation? Was there in fact such a thing as a benign, innocent backrub? But when her hand came to rest on my leg, I knew I was not misreading the situation. Slowly, I started working her sides, edging carefully down toward her pelvis and back up toward breasts, my hand a scoop, a diver of all things forbidden. Very tricky territory, here. If it was innocent, if I was indeed misreading the situation, I would soon know it. Closer and closer I massaged her sides when, finally, she rose slightly onto her elbows so I could move my hands over her breasts. Her eyes were closed. Her breathing audible.

It was on.

College sex! Dorm Sex! Is there anything better between two willing young people? I had never before in my life been the kind of guy who landed the tall brunette on the front row of English class, and yet there I was. I was large! I contained multitudes! Did it bother me that she had slept with Mark before? Did it bother me that I was second banana on the tree of sex? Did it bother me that there was no talk of a relationship astew, that what we were engaging in was a classic episode of afternoon delight? Further, did it bother me that from then on, our code for doing it was, "Can I borrow your Bob Marley tape?" And that even after we had crazy, Anne-grabbing-the towel-rack-on-my-closet-while-I-went-to-work-from-behind-sex, she also had sex again with Mark?

Are you kidding?

And what can be said here for Anne? Nothing other than to say she was wicked smart, assertive, and clearly enjoyed the stringless romp between friends, and, in our case, roommates. The freedom! The beauty of it all! This was what the college experience was all about!

I loved college! What else would explain my failing grades? I loved too much.

The end of that term came by way of flames. But first came the party at our unofficial fraternity house (large enough only to house six or so seniors, hence why I was still in the dorms). At the party, Anne and I disappeared into a bathroom where we could have locked-in-the-bathroom party sex.

What happened later that night I learned the next morning when I staggered back to my room, and to what was, by that point, a dispersing public spectacle. I hadn't connected the smallish fire truck in the parking lot of Juniper Hall with anything related to C-219, my room. But I was the only one who had not made such connections. What I learned was this: At some point late in the night, Anne caught a ride back to the dorms, where she made a late-night visit to our room for a midnight rendezvous with Mark. There, they found themselves drunk, naked, and humping. Because Mark was Mark, sultry martini music murmured from the James Bond soundtrack, and several candles were throwing the room into a shimmering fun house of shadow. Then just after they passed out naked in bed, one candle's flame started licking the curtain. And when the curtain caught fire, it fell on the desks, catching papers on fire, and so on. Smoke, alarms, and flames woke the dreamy couple. Everyone in the hall had stepped from their rooms only to glimpse Anne—naked save a towel wrapped around her—poking her head out with assurances: "Everything is fine, everything is fine." This even as smoke poured from the room in clouds, and as a naked Mark was swatting out the flames with his pillow.

What I found that morning was Mark, hung-over, and the charred remains of schoolwork that wouldn't have been completed anyway. We had been put on notice. Even though I was absent, I was still an accomplice. They searched our room and found alcohol. And Anne had been in our room past 11:00, clearly a violation. Clearly out-of-bounds in this small, conservative backwater.

It wasn't a kind time. I was certain that my run in college had just ended, and in many ways it had. This finality was evidenced, it seemed, in the blackened remnants on my desk, and the poofy comforter which had partly melted at the edge.

So this is how things end. In fire. Erasure. I had been kicked out of the dorms. I was nineteen, penniless, and had taken a couch in our unofficial fraternity house as my new home. I needed a job. I was failing out of school. And Mark and I had started to part ways, not because of anything specific, but just because that is what happens between freshman year roommates. You are best friends, mates, confidants, and then time blows through in a gust, and just like that you are acquaintances. You surrender to this ebb and flow of social patterns the way you surrender to a new story, a new book that washes up on the shores of your life.

Another kind of surrender occurred one night at a party not long after I started couch crashing. I don't recall where I was, and it doesn't matter, but I do remember running into Milo, an acquaintance with crazy curly hair that stuck straight up off the top of his head. He was wry and sarcastic and was infatuated with Ayn Rand in the cerebrally frenetic way Ayn Rand fans are (i.e., put two of them in a room and mention her name and come back six days later, etc.). But he was also a writer and, I had just learned, a Hemingway devotee.

"Hemingway?" I called over the noise of the party.

"He's fan-fucking-tastic!"

"Old man Santiago and shit?"

He became impatient with me. "No, no, no," he said. "The short stories, man. Read the short stories."

I wasn't persuaded and it showed. He held his beer bottle out and while issuing his index finger, meaning, "hang on a second." He slipped through the tangled mass of partygoers and came back with a friend. "Peter," he said. "Tell Brandon about Hemingway's short stories."

"Fan-fucking-tastic," he said.

I laughed, and took a belt of beer. Why, I asked, was he so great?

And there ensued banter between the two of them about dialogue and image and they seemed to be in a race to name their next in a long string of favorite stories. "'Up in Michigan,'" they said. "Oh, shit, and you *have* to read 'The Three Day Blow,'" they said. "And 'The Short Happy Life of Francis MacComber.' Holy fucking shit. You *have* to read that."

It was the first time I had ever been to a party that involved a discussion of literature or writing. Something electric coursed through my body, and the intensity of feeling that the conversation had sparked was enhanced by the alcohol, and I felt surer about this place we call the world than I had ever felt before. In the end, I was persuaded to read Hemingway because of their enthusiasm alone.

"Come over next week," Milo said. "We stay up late and drink whiskey and write and read The Man."

I was all in, and we shook on it.

A few days later, I found myself loafing around town on a heedless afternoon beneath a crushing blue sky. This was spring 1992, shortly after my arrest in Moccasin, Arizona. I had dropped out of college after two quarters. There comes a point of no return, about halfway through a term, when the guilt of failure is magnified in direct proportion to the futility of reversing course, of academic redemption. Beyond that, there comes a general disconnect, an abstractness that assuages the mind. And beyond that, college just becomes an idea, something other people do. Hence the triple zero GPA. But on that afternoon, I had ten dollars in my pocket—my only ten dollars, as it happened—and decided to blow it on a used copy of Hemingway's short stories rather than a twelve-pack of beer. I took the paperback to a coffee shop where I spent the remaining change from my ten on a coffee and a day-old pastry.

Who was that young man in that coffee shop that afternoon,

and what was he feeling? A strange creature, lean and quiet, he is apologetic in his countenance. It's a tricky business cracking open our younger selves for a peek inside, especially in vulnerable moments (is there such a thing as an invulnerable moment, ever?). I remember sitting in that coffee shop. I remember its name—The Dog & Duck, and the owner's annoying shtick he employed whenever someone left. Instead of hollering "Thanks! Come again!" he belted out, "Aarf, aarf! Quack, quack!" I remember that and my irritation. But I liked the high ceilings and the brick walls, and the books piled pell-mell on rickety bookcases. And, besides, it was the only coffee shop in that Mormondominated town (recall that the Latter-day Saints do not drink coffee). There I sat, broke, with a copy of Hemingway's stories. The college flunky. The dropout. It's a wonder I bought the book at all. It's a wonder I took the time to read it. It's a wonder how I fell into those pages. But I did. First in that coffee shop, and then in the days and weeks and months and years that came afterward.

Put another way, I surrendered to this author and his stories. Like so many people, I was leveled by his economy. It took time, of course, to even glimpse what he was up to on the page, to even arrive at that word—economy. It took afternoons in the coffee shop, and it took nights at Milo's house drinking bottom-shelf whiskey and smoking cigarettes and reading and hitting the typewriter keys (yes: I had my mother's electric Smith Corona typewriter) on my own scraps of paper to see it, but eventually, I started to. His nouns seemed to fall to the page like anvils—decided and forceful. Here were unpretentious verbs. See the dialogue firing like pistons. Milo was right. What wasn't to admire?

It's no astute observation to say that Hemingway was a complicated man, a complicated author who complicated our sense of American literature in the best sense. But he was complicated to me personally. Like so many would-be writers, I became a follower, a sorrowful imitator, a Son of Papa. I wanted his style to be my style, and slowly convinced myself that his style was my style. So there I parked the bearded saint, up on the Great Pillar of Literature. If studying his prose rhythms in private at the coffee shop (between "Aarf, aarf!" and "Quack, quack!") helped me in some remote, desert-island kind of way (and I believe it did), my obsession over the man himself wasn't as useful. Was in fact destructive. "The man drank like more than any author in history, and look at what he wrote!" Milo said one night while pouring us another round. "And he didn't even go to college. The son of a bitch did it on his own!"

We clinked glasses and threw the whiskey down the hatch. That night and for so many nights afterward, we drank to The Man.

In other words, there exists a kind of danger when you introduce a certain brand of young man to the words of Hemingway. If literature is the great vicarious second version of our dreams, fears, and pities, then to live vicariously through Hemingway can prove to be a wreckful ambition, or at least it did with me.

BUT OF COURSE you know it's foolish, these thoughts. OF COURSE you wouldn't be caught dead uttering them aloud. OF COURSE you know where books end and where you begin. OF COURSE.

And yet.

And yet the chorus in the young man's mind drones on in no less convincing a rhythm than the rhythm of Papa's prose itself:

If Hemingway didn't go to college
If Hemingway could drink like this
If this is what Hemingway did
If this is the Hemingway code, then by God
If he did it on his own, then by God

The young man who carries this forlorn song in his head isn't stupid, isn't some dolt. No. He knows better. His only crime is innocence. His only crime is the haunting desire to find himself and the words that illuminate, and to double expose his place in the world. His only crime, therefore, is love. Love for the words that came before him, measured out across the prairies and tundra of the human imagination like fence lines. Love for story. Love for the printed, paper-in-hand page, the raw material that reveals the secret you, the exquisite wreck of humanity. Of these crimes, he is guilty. Guilty before he knows they are crimes at all.

The more I read of Hemingway, the more I fell into the maelstrom of influence. From the short stories, I moved on to *The Sun Also Rises*, and it was with this book that I learned how to type, learned really how to get that Smith Corona to sing its song. (In high school, I had been advised to take shop classes rather than typing classes.) I had by this point graduated from the couch in our unofficial house and secured a bedroom. A small space, but perfect for me. It was all bed and a small desk on which I parked the typewriter, that motor mouth of a machine. I decided that if I wanted to write I needed to learn how to type—a more useful skill than lighting things on fire and shooting hunks of wood across the shop. And so I practiced by typing the opening lines of SAR: "Robert Cohn was once middleweight boxing champion of Princeton. Do not think that I am very much impressed by that as a boxing title, but it meant a lot to Cohn." I had gotten the idea from some other writer, of course, and was imitating an imitation of the real thing, the true "gen." Eventually, though, I could type 60 WPM and felt a warm satisfaction at hearing the keys clacking against the paper, of seeing the story—however bad (and it was bad, each and every one)—lift itself out of its own primordial dream.

There is a way in which Hemingway is necessary to a young writer, and even more so to a particular kind of young writer who is male and from some rural backwater where slicing open the white belly of a trout or slitting the hot, coarse throat of a mule deer in winter are rites tantamount to religion. I could take his books home, in other words. There existed no betrayal in availing myself to his vision. Couched in crasser terms, Hemingway was a man's man, and the big-truck construction workers who were crowbar tough could appreciate/identify with/understand my enthusiasm for Hemingway even if they had never read him. There was, then, a kind of redemption to be found in this acceptance. So Hemingway mattered to me not just because he was a writer and because I perceived his example as granting a kind of permission for misbehavior, but also because I could retain in a foot in the world I had forsaken (or at least risked forsaking). He was an anchor, and as long as I had Hemingway, I had a way back home.

Consider the visit I made home during spring break of the spring quarter in which I was not enrolled. I had caught a ride with a hippie friend from Cedar City to Logan, Utah, where he lived, and from there, my grandmother picked me up and brought me home to Soda Springs. (My parents had recently purchased a fifth-wheel trailer and were wheeling around the country, hopping from one union job to another where my dad could make a high wage scale as an electrician). Tucked in my army-issue duffle was *The Sun Also Rises*. I spent the days lounging around my grandmother's house, watching TV and reading Hemingway. At night I would drink beer, smoke a bowl on the back step, and scribble in my notebooks. How is school? People would ask.

Great, I'd say. I'm reading Hemingway over the break.

Hemingway, eh? They'd say, their eyebrows lifting. I've always liked Hemingway, they'd say.

Yeah. You should read his short stories, I'd say. They're fantastic.

Once or twice at night I would meet a few high school friends who had either stayed in Soda Springs or who had also returned for spring break, and we would drag Main Street, rekindling the old machinations of youth: driving up and down our one and only thoroughfare, drinking beer, and flirting with dreamy-eyed, curfew-breaking, nubile hometown girls. We would find our way out to Piss Holler where we could piss and holler. On these nights I would wear my Delta Sigma Chi sweatshirt and too much

Giorgio cologne. I would flash my college smile and talk books and writing and, especially, Hemingway. Too embarrassed that I had dropped out, had in fact, flunked out, had been booted from the dorms, had been arrested, that everything had gone up in smoke, I avoided the topic of *School* entirely, and talked instead about the parties we threw, the glorious world beyond Caribou County and that sagebrush land. I was walking too tall in jeans I couldn't afford and trying to cash in on the fiction I had made for myself: that I was some golden boy returned home from the Bright Lights and Big City of College Life, that I was the stars-and-stripes fraternity boy stepping off his westbound train from his eastern Ivy League daydream that I was the soldier home from wars thundering on across vast oceans. How simple it is for fictions to beget fictions. How foolishly simple.

But how difficult it is to drive our heroes away, to toss them from the citadel of creation. It would take many years of reading his books, of studying his stories, of going fishing in the rain with too much wine, and then many more years of not reading his books, and unreading his stories, of unraveling the mythos, to discern the boundaries between his words and my own. That younger version of me, the smart-mouthed dropout, was too empty, too adrift, and too innocent to call the bearded saint down from his pillar and lose that voice.

Hinton, S. E. *The Outsiders.* New York: Laurel Leaf, 1968.

In the seventh grade my literal voice was cracking with embarrassing frequency. I was gangly and awkward and had just been prescribed glasses. It was during this year that I had become aware, if only vaguely, that my family wasn't like those I read about or saw on television. We didn't do ski trips, The Lake, or Orlando. We never used *summer* as a verb. The books lying around our house were of the variety that merely entertained: fat, grocery-store paperbacks with lurid titles and covers. Mysteries and true crime and horror. In our world, the days and months and seasons were containers to be filled with work and work alone. A line had been drawn not between daydreams and the here and now, but between other kids whose families retreated to their cabins and those of us who wore long hair and heavy-metal tee-shirts that said it all: "If it's too loud, you're too old."

So when Ms. Garrison, my seventh grade English teacher, passed around a book called *The Outsiders,* I felt my world lift a little. Here was one of the few assigned books I enjoyed. She told us to think about the title, to consider this book as a tale of those with and those without, and then shot me a steady glance and said, "I think you'll like it."

Of course I loved it. But, as always, I loved it for all the wrong reasons. I didn't merely sympathize with Johnny, Soda Pop, Pony Boy, et al., I *empathized* with them. And here it gets strange because while we were working class, we weren't poor by any means, and, most of all, my parents were *alive* unlike Pony Boy's. So the basis of my empathy was false and self-serving. I wanted to be poorer, more troubled, and badder than I was. In short, I wanted to be an Outsider. I convinced myself that I understood that world of denim and switchblades and sneakers and long, oiled hair. I had convinced myself of it so thoroughly that I started to look like a character from the book. And so did a few friends. We wore our Levi jackets and denim jeans and I carried a butterfly knife in my back pocket. We traded in our glasses for contacts, smoked cigarettes, and wore cynicism like a new skin.

I remember wanting to live in a city, to have real alleys to prowl and to stake out as my own. To have territory and what people called "street smarts." But we only had so many streets in my rural Idaho hometown, so "street smarts" were, by virtue of diminished geography, three traffic lights, and a semaphore, hard to come by. Our town did have one honest-to-goodness alley, which was behind the movie theatre. It was a place of macadam and cement and bricks and cinderblock walls and broken bottle glass and medallion-like puddles ringed with the oil-slick colors of the rainbow. So we called that our place. It suited us. There we could exhale drags of blue smoke, kick a brick wall, and spout backward, in-grown teenage maxims like, "This town blows," or "Preppies are gay." And if I ever doubted our proclamations, I needed only to go to *The Outsiders* to see a hardened, cruel world mirrored back to me. Becoming an Outsider was an easy and satisfying way of exacting contradistinction, of drawing a line between realms. In other words, I had entered the world of fiction, casting myself as its lead character.

How odd, then, that only one year later—in the eighth grade—when I had, of my own accord, moved on to Hinton's other books like *Rumblefish* and *Tex*, my parents were called into the school for a meeting about my performance in my English class.

"We're concerned," the counselor said. "We're worried that Brandon isn't going to be ready for high school English."

My mother, while having only a high school diploma and six months of trade-school to her credit, excelled in English and was an avid reader. Her favorite teachers had been English teachers and so, in her mind, it followed that my experience would be the same, regardless of my tepid grades. "What do you mean?" she demanded.

"He is behind the rest of his peers," he said, shoving some paperwork across his desk, paperwork that cited, among other things, standardized testing data, national averages, state averages, and, finally, my scores. "So we are recommending that he enter remedial English with our special resources teacher."

Despite my mother's protests, I was, after that meeting, catapulted into a storage closet they called remedial English. For something like fifty minutes a day, four or five of us—all boys and one girl—ran basic grammar drills and filled out colorful, childlike worksheets that helped us identify parts of speech and tense issues. Mrs. Gibbs, our resource teacher, was a tall and kind woman who exuded the very air of patience, as if she had been training all her life to help these children in the sticks learn how to park their periods in the right place. The whole gig felt like a waste of time, and so most of us would tell fart jokes or tease the one girl among us.

Ultimately, I ran the drills, though. I parked my periods in the right places. I hung my apostrophes from the right trees. And I got my nouns and verbs to make friends. All the while, Mrs. Gibbs would pat me on the shoulder and issue praise, encouragement. Soon, she put me in charge of helping the others. Once, on a wintry afternoon, Mrs. Gibbs spotted my copy of *Rumblefish*. "Which class is this for?" She asked, picking it up.

"It's not for any class," I said with a shrug. "I'm just reading it. It's a cool story."

I could feel the other resource students staring at me while she issued more praise, and my face turned red and so I changed the subject.

On another such afternoon, while goofing off in our storage closet, I called one of the kids a morphodite. After our session was out, Mrs. Gibbs asked me to stay a moment. "You know the most interesting words!" she said. "I'm beginning to wonder why you are in here."

That I didn't know what morphodite even meant, and that I had cribbed it from *Stand by Me* (as in, "Gordy, go get the provisions you morphodite,") didn't seem to matter.

Not long after, Mrs. Gibbs made some appeals on my behalf, and I was excused from having to take remedial English. I hadn't proved myself as some kind of grammar whiz (indeed, much of the English language was by turns baffling and boring), so much as I had proved that I didn't belong in that storage closet. So I accepted the switch with a shrug, thankful that it was one less thing I had to do.

Hornby, Nick. *High Fidelity*. New York: Riverhead, 1995.

This is the book you read when you are a man and your love life goes south. This is the book of consolation. This is the book that puts a voice in your ear telling you that the world won't fly off its axis. That you will survive the wounds, the dirty kick to the guts she dealt you. This is the book that says it's fine to get piss drunk and scream at the top of your lungs in the middle of a midnight boulevard, because fuck it—she left and what else are you gonna do? This is the book that grants permission for the young man to admit, to utter, to say, to dare speak such a sappy word as *heartache*. This is a book for men coming to terms with what it means to be a man, and to that extent, this book was invaluable for me.

Keep the sucker in your back pocket.
Under your pillow.
On the car seat.
Back of the toilet.
It's a lifesaver, this one.

It was my friend Levi who recommended it. He was a tall, broad shouldered business major with Montana roots and Jack Kerouac hair. He smoked a lot, one of the true lovers of the cigarette, one of the people who just look cooler for their smoking. He was also an obsessive reader, which, in my limited experience of hanging out with business majors, was rare. He read everything. And he seemed to have his finger on the pulse of American culture in a way that baffled me. He was always in-the-know, never not in-the-know, and

I liked hanging out with him because he was a reader and someone whose in-the-knowness would, I hoped, rub off on me.

I got around to the book on his recommend sometime in the
spring of 1997. "You need to read *High Fidelity*," he said one afternoon. We were on break at the telemarketing company we
worked for and we were smoking. Cigarettes never appealed to
me, really, unless I was hanging out with Levi, and then I
bummed them continuously. I hadn't heard of the book and
Levi had. This was the nature of our conversations: Levi appris-
ing me of the things I didn't know, and me scribbling titles down
not on a receipt, but on a notepad. But there was something in
his tone, in the way he worked the word *need*, in how he took his
time with that word as a way of saying, "Look, man. I know you're
all busted up, but you've got to get it together. I mean, look at
you!" I was a wreck. I hadn't shaved in weeks. I was gaining
weight. I had a gash on my chin because I had fallen down drunk
and split it open on a curb. I was drinking in the morning, afternoon, night, morning, afternoon night. I took beers into the
shower. Had beers—or, when the budget was flush—Bloody
Marys with/for breakfast. And all of this after a fairly good run,
academically speaking. I was back in school (and had been for
some time) and I was doing well (for me) if you consider my
transcripts from that previous spring and fall quarters. To wit:

SPRING QUARTER 1996

ENGL—333	AM LITERATURE: MODERN	C+
SPAN—102	ELEM SPANISH II	B
	CURRENT GPA	2.689
	CUMULATIVE GPA	2.093

FALL QUARTER 1996

ART—101	ART APPRECIATION	C—
ENGL—447	THE ROMANTIC AGE	B—
ENGL—474	SHAKESPEARE: TRAGEDIES	B—
PSY—	GENERAL PSYCHOLOGY	B
	CURRENT GPA	2.606
	CUMULATIVE GPA	2.178

But that is when I was in crazy, lose-your-head love. I'd met this girl at work––at the telemarketing company I had been working at for four years. When I went to work for Monarch (not its real name), the industry was in its golden age, its roaring heyday. This was before caller ID. Pre iPhone. Before automated and predictive dialers. Before entire call centers were boxed up and outsourced to Bangalore. And, most notably, it was before the National Do-Not-Call Registry. And I was there, on the phones, five, sometimes six, days a week. After a year of calling, I was promoted to Quality Control. Then I became a supervisor. I gave high-energy seminars on voice quality and a concept I created: "The Three C's of Call Control: Confidence, Credibility, and Composure." I wore a tie every day. I acquired a whole new lexicon of terms: contribution margin, billable hours, client monitoring, business casual. If there was one thing I knew, and I knew little, it was the industry. I watched its very landscape change dramatically. I saw the manual phones carted out one day under a swatch of desert sky and dumpstered while new dialers arrived in a fury of winking lights. I saw the impact of Caller ID, and watched the business buck against this technology. I saw it all.

But another thing I saw, was this girl, Mary—a real looker. She was a trainee in a group of thirty or so newbies, and I had been sent in, as I always was, to deliver the Quality Control speech. I told them how they needed to stay on script (knowing full well they would break this rule, or at least the good ones would). I told them how my department would listen to and sometimes record their conversations. And I told them how to make sales. I made them laugh. And occasionally, I would make eye contact with Mary. And she with me. Later, in my department, I would tell Levi: "This chick," I said. "She's got the *bedroom eyes*." I was into her in a big way.

At the time, I had been whoring around like so many roving, hard-drinking frat boys are wont to do. There was some protected sex. But mostly unprotected sex. Foolish sex, in other words. The usual array of one-nighters. I had come a long way from that tentative creature in the dorms. I had come a long way since the days when I was simply "Mark's Roommate." Mark had fled north years earlier and the shadow had fled with the man. Confidence grew in me like a weed, wild and invasive. I wore J. Crew. I drove a Toyota Land Cruiser. I wore a heavy watch, plenty of cologne, and wrote a weekly column for our school newspaper, *The University Journal.* I had turned into one of those old-school Sigma Nus I had been been intimidated by.

I had invented a whole new life for myself. If I were to compare my younger selves, pluck two of me from different periods of my past—the Brandon of the heavy metal band days, say, and this one, and put them side by side, what might I learn? Which one is the real Brandon? Which one is a fiction? Can I recognize them? Can they recognize one another? Does the imposter lurk in the past, or is he running the show in the present? Witness the long-haired, dangly-skull-earringed rocker with a Metallica wallet. Now witness this guy who seems to have stepped out of a catalogue of the upwardly mobile or off the page of a novel. What can you see? Looking at it now, I see some kind of necessary sadness that accompanies the hunger of climbing up. It is such a desperate race, rewriting the future as a way of erasing, or at least, revising the past, your place, your kin, your blood. But if I am totally honest, too, I will admit the thrill of it all. There is a thrill in reinvention, a freedom. Because whatever I was doing, it was paying off. I was named Magister, or pledge marshal, of our fraternity (which had by that point gained a national charter through Sigma Chi). My grades were fine. I wrote a column that people read. And I had plenty of girls. So why not follow the catalog version of me? After all, it was this version that won Mary over.

But it was the real me who drove her away. Seen this way, fictions have their consequences.

In terms of college romance, we were solid. Ours was a months-long relationship. At night, after sex, we would scheme and daydream about our future. We will live in San Francisco! And go sailing! And we will be the cool parents who let our sixteen-year-old son have a beer on the sailboat! We will restore an old home in the Bay Area! We will make millions! I would write great books. She would head up an ad agency. The glittering future was right there before us, luminescent and tangible. Just reach out and snatch it up.

But oh, how the dreams give way.

One morning as I was leaving for my job at Monarch Marketing, we'd had a massive blow-up. The night before, we had gone grocery shopping. We unloaded the shopping bags from my Land Cruiser into the kitchen of my fraternity house. I hadn't shut the rear driver's side door all the way. That morning, a desert wintry cold front hung in the darkness, and I was running late. That is when I discovered my battery was dead. Another tardy slip at Monarch Marketing would spell all kinds of trouble, would mean I would get written up. I was raging around the house in the blue light of early dawn. "It's a brand new battery!" I roared.

Then Mary said, "It was probably because you didn't shut your door all the way."

I spun around and looked at her, fuming. "What?"

"You didn't shut the door all the way and the dome light was on."

"You saw it and didn't say anything?"

"I thought you wanted it like that for a reason."

I stood before her in disbelief. "What are you talking about?"

"I was afraid to say anything."

Then I blew. More yelling. More hollering. And the house shook.

One night at a dance, I started drinking the "Mad Jack" edition of Yukon Jack. A friend had it out in his car, and we played the my-bottle-your-bottle back and forth drinking game. Mary and I had drunk some wine at dinner before the dance and I had quickly become smashed. So smashed, in fact, that I had been hauled out of the dance by two security guards. Mary followed me out, and a gaggle of fraternity brothers followed her. A fight erupted and Mary slapped me. I stood there beneath the fall moon swaying and smarting and watched her stomp off into the darkness. "Bitch!" I yelled.

"Come on, Schrand," Dan said. "Let's get you home."

"Fuck you." I stagger-stepped from the sidewalk into the middle of the street.

Two or three guys trailed behind. "Schrand! Let's go."

That's when I shoved Dan and he shoved me back, and then I shoved him, and then he shoved me, and I collapsed in the street. I lay there, eyes filled with sweat, moon, whiskey, and hate, and then I grabbed his leg and bit—yes, *bit*—dog-like, Tyson-like, one solid rabid clamp down on his calf.

"Oh, shit, he's biting!"

Two guys shook me loose and dragged me, the drunken wreck of a rag doll, through the street and dumped me in a car. "You're going home, fucker."

The next morning, Mary calls. "We need to talk."

My head is pounding. "Yeah," I croak. "Sure."

We talk it through as we have talked through many fights. She apologizes for slapping me. I apologize for being me, and then we let it go. A few days blow by and we're fine again. Meanwhile, Dan won't talk to me. Won't return my calls, and I feel like shit. He's the closest thing to a best friend I've got, and I've gone and fucked that up too. He is silent for weeks, and then a month passes before he breaks. We're at a party and I say, *Hey*, and we hash it out. "You need to get your shit together, Schrand," he scolds. "Look at you. Christ."

I look away into the middle-distance, into the crowd of party-goers. Then I nod. "I know. I know." And I do know. But what you know and what you do don't always serve the same interest.

About a month later, another fight. The fight to end all fights. At a party, Mary is flirting openly with Dan. Sitting on his lap, arm around his neck, sipping from his drink. A girl approaches me and whispers in my ear, "What's up with Mary?"

And I say, loud enough to draw everyone's attention, "I HAVE NO IDEA WHAT'S UP WITH MARY. MAYBE WE SHOULD ASK MARY WHAT'S UP WITH MARY!"

Mary's face goes slack and she slides off Dan's lap and leaves.

Someone from kitchen, whispers, "*Awkward . . .*"

Slowly, the partiers return to their partying, and I go outside to look for Mary. She's standing beneath a tree in the front yard. "Let's go home," she says.

I agree and ask someone to drive us home. I am silent the entire way. She is silent the entire way, and the driver is silent too. All these silences. Silences before the crashing glass, silences before the whole fucking thing comes down in shards.

In my room at the fraternity house, we get into it big time. "What the fuck was that?" I roar.

"What was what?"

"You fucking know what. Dan: that's what."

"Your friends can be my friends, too, Brandon. Grow up."

"There's a difference between friends and wanting to fuck them."

"Did it ever occur to you that maybe I was trying to get your attention?"

"What the fuck is that supposed to mean?" I say.

"It means that party after party, you disappear with your frat brothers and I'm stuck talking to someone I barely know."

"It sure looks like you know Dan."

She pauses. Then: "It's like you don't want to be seen with me."

"Whatever."

She gets up to leave and I grab her wrist. "Let go of me!" She shakes loose.

"You just going to run away?" I shout.

"From you, yes."

She then tells me we're through, that it's been a long time coming, and then I blow.

This time it's not Mary who slaps me. It's the other way around. I slap her. It happens so fast and it cannot be undone. Will never, in fact, be undone.

"You drunk!" she cries and leaves.

Standing outside my door is another fraternity brother, who could hear the argument, the shouting, this kind of undoing. When Mary pushed past him, he stared right into me. There was nothing left to say. I had disgraced myself in such a way that words couldn't undo what I had done. So he went back to my room and we never spoke about that night.

From my journal the next day: "Who am I becoming? Who am I afraid of?" Answer: I was afraid of myself, afraid that the monster within who was capable of such malice was the real Brandon, and the other, outer-Brandon, was an empty shell, a catalog image, a fiction.

As you can guess, I tried to call Mary many times to apologize, and as you can guess, her roommates rightly kept me at bay. "Brandon," they'd say in steely voices. "We have told you to *stop calling.* There is nothing you can say to change anything. So let's leave it at that, okay?"

"I just want to apologize."

"If you care about her, you'll leave her alone."

"I am NOT that kind of person," I'd insist, my voice quavering. Hand gripping the phone cord.

A pause.

And then, "Stop calling."

Then: click.

I can only imagine what they must have been thinking. They were thinking: *bad guy.* Bad news. Stay the hell away from him. And they were right to think those things. Of course I hated them for their gate-keeper, stonewalling tactics at the time, for forging that kind of confederacy against me, for protecting her from the ugly thing I had done. For who I had suddenly become. I hated them because I couldn't get past myself.

There are in this world the unforgivable things.

There are in this world the leagues of boys who try to become men but become something else entirely along the way. Something they can't even recognize. A stranger in the mirror with a lurker's blood. An intruder's heart. You catch your reflection on water, on the dark windows of an office building, and you freeze that image in your mind—the slightly hunched figure, the hollow gaze—and you know that it is no longer you, but someone else, and you wonder if there could be anything more terrifying than that.

The breakup occurred just at the end of the term, and despite my dark misery and lunacy and self-hate, I had eked out another quarter. I had been doing well in my Hemingway/Faulkner course that quarter, which, in some foolish ways, contributed to marathon binge drinking, which, in turn, contributed to the breakup. If I wasn't hanging out with Dan, I was usually with Spenser, another fraternity brother with whom I had much in common. We were English majors, one-time roommates, Jimmy Buffett fans (how, really, does one leap from Metallica to Margaritaville in a single bound?). And we each had lines from the *Blues Brothers* and *Caddyshack* memorized. Because we were both in the Hemingway/Faulkner class, and because we both were heavy drinkers, we spent our nights throwing small gatherings at his house where we drank boxed wine (or Space Pigs, as we called them on account of the snoutish nozzle and foil bag) and talked like Hemingway wrote. "The wine is good and it is red and true!" And "Are you tight? Because I am quite tight and it is good to be tight and true!" And so on. So even in the face of the breakup with Mary, my GPA survived intact, for the most part.

WINTER QUARTER 1997

ENGL—332	AMER LIT MIDDLE PERIOD	B+
ENGL—464	HEMINGWAY & FAULKNER	A
POSC—	AMERICAN NATIONAL GVRNMT	D−
	CURRENT GPA	2.515
	CUMULATIVE GPA	2.218

As if a prophecy, my grades that semester spelled out BAD. And things were bad. But it would only get worse. I signed up for new classes, one of which was a fiction writing class. I was going to write a novel. A great novel that reconciled my past and would deal with my heartache and fear. So I decided to write about a trailer park. And I would title it, boringly, "Trailer Park."

When I was in the fifth grade we lived for a short time in a single-wide trailer in Idaho Falls, Idaho, where my dad was picking up electrical work at the Idaho National Engineering Laboratory in the Idaho desert. I would spend my days wearing camouflage pants, pretending I was in the A-Team, and I took great pleasure at stomping in mud puddles and whacking metal things with a stick. So I drew on that chapter of youth for material. But my parents were, at the time of my writing my novel, living in a squalid trailer court behind the Boulder Station Casino in Las Vegas. (My dad was one of the many electricians working on the MGM Grand.) The gravel road that snaked through the park was pocked with puddles of filthy water, and broken bottle glass glinted here and there, and fast food wrappers cartwheeled through the park in sudden desert gusts. My parents had become friends with a crack addict named Caroline who had a young boy. My mother felt sorry for the boy and so she would help Caroline. A little dab of money. Fresh-baked bread. Some help cleaning her trailer. A ride to the food bank, her parole officer. And so on. Going on nearly thirty years sober, my mother has long felt the pangs of guilt for living such a romping lifestyle when I young, and ever since, she has taken quiet routes to what she sees as redemption or atonement for her years as a too-young, trial-and-error mother. Some of those routes led to me. Some would eventually lead to my own children. But while they hunkered down in the trailer park behind the Boulder Station Casino, while tumbleweeds clung to the skirting of their fifth-wheel trailer in a run-down park, the route that was most immediate was the one that led to Caroline and her boy.

It followed, then, that as a social climber who fancied himself a writer I would co-opt Caroline and her son's story for my fiction writing class. In the book I named her Carolina and her son Code (I forget what his real name was). Other primary characters who lived in the trailer park included a woman named

Susan, based entirely on my mother; a plumber and unlikely literary man, Jerry (named after my biological father); and Pastor Williams. I stole the novel's structure from *As I Lay Dying*, so each chapter was told from the perspective of the various characters in the book. Mostly typed single-spaced, the novel was patently bad, but I was determined if nothing else.

Late at night, I typed. Yes, we had computer labs on campus. And yes, by 1997 most people had their own computers. And yes, it would have made more sense to write my novel on a computer. But I didn't. Instead, I clackity-clacked away on the Smith Corona electric typewriter. My room in the Sigma Chi house was large, and two of the walls were all windows. I built a long bench and parked my typewriter there where I would have a view outside. I felt like a writer. And part of feeling like a writer entailed drinking discount, plastic-bottle Green Stripe blended scotch while I wrote. The trouble there is, every time I took a drink mid-paragraph, say, I would set the tumbler to the right of the humming motor-mouth, and when I hit return, the carriage would knock over my drink with a great ka-thunk! Scotch would spill everywhere, and I would cuss and clean up the mess and fan the wet pages and consciously, ever so consciously, set my tumbler on the left side. Soon, however, it would return to the right side, and it would be ka-thunk! all over again. I was convinced that I could write my way out of misery, but all I was doing was drinking myself deeper. It's an old story, a sad and empty story, but it was a true story all the same.

And here is a side effect of that story:

ENGL—252	INTRO TO DRAMA	F
ENGL—353	WORLD LIT: MODERN	A—
ENGL—409	FICTION WRITING	F
SPAN—ELEM	SPANISH III	UW
	CURRENT GPA	0.925
	CUMULATIVE GPA	2.053

I was twenty-four years old. A man-boy. Mostly boy. The man in me scratched out an A in my modern world literature course. The boy waved the white flag of surrender in my other classes. I recall one day specifically. I had a Spanish exam and I had been up all night at my typewriter and had drunk an entire pint of the Green Stripe. The next morning Spenser rapped at my door. I woke fully clothed in my bed. My shirt, pants, and sheets were soaking wet with sweat. Spenser waved his hand through the boozy stench in the air. "Jesus, dude. It smells like a bar in here. You all right?" I wasn't all right. But we had an exam in twenty minutes. So Spenser hauled me to Spanish. I was pale and shaking and smelled sour like death and booze. Halfway through the exam, my instructor sidled up next to me. "Are you okay?" She asked. She knew. Oh, she knew. She knew that there is nothing funny at all about alcohol poisoning.

Meanwhile, enough time had passed after my breakup with Mary, that she finally took a phone call from me. Then another. And another. For a brief interval, I tried to win her back by reading her excerpts from *Trailer Park*. Reading to her was a dumb, self-absorbed idea, really, but writing had wooed other girls in the past, and Rob in Hornby's *High Fidelity* wooed girls with mix tapes (as I also had in high school), so why wouldn't this work? The failed reasoning, the logic gone to termites, the thinking wrecked with misery. The brutality of wishful thinking. Put another way, I was a brooding, glum, and tortured young man, all a-blubber and busted up over our falling out, and I would cry while I read passages of this god-awful novel to her. How she didn't break out laughing is beyond me. Instead, she just sat beside me on my bed, statuesque and porcelain-cool. In truth, I didn't want her back. I was just as much done with our snarled chemistry as she was. What I wanted is what all guys want when abandoned: I wanted to have sex one more time. Mostly I wanted to have sex because I always wanted to have sex, but I also wanted to have sex because, the reasoning went, if she was having sex with me, it meant that she wasn't having sex with someone else. Or at least not right at that moment, and for juvenile reasons, I saw this reasoning as somehow Therapeutic.

Also filed under *T* for *therapeutic* was *High Fidelity.* When I hit this line in Hornby's tour de force (and it is a TDF for any guy who has sustained the kind of seismic shock Rob has in the book), I knew I wasn't alone: "But in my fearful imaginings Charlie was as abandoned and as noisy as any character in a porn film. She was Marco's plaything, she responded to his every touch with shrieks of orgasmic delight. No woman in the history of the world had better sex than the sex Charlie had with Marco in my head."

Oh my fucking god! I remember thinking. That's it! Here is the male's psyche laid bare on the page! Here is ultimate vulnerability! Here is fear and heartache. This is what it feels like in the dark places of your dungeon mind! And yes, it's okay to say heartache because Rob is feeling it and he is no slouch in the Manly department and because Hornby wrote it this way. Hornby gave me permission to express grief—haunting, reeling, high-wire grief.

Not feeling alone is important in this stage of wallowing. And the opportunity to laugh (not at what you have done, but Rob has done). *High Fidelity* came to the rescue on both fronts. It was my support group, my therapy, my yurt, my tranquilizer, my 12-step program, my serenity, my laugh-track, and, finally, my redemption. Is that heavy handed—redemption? For some, perhaps. But not for me. The soul I walked around in was an invented soul, a tried-on soul, a feared soul—three-fourths novel and one-fourth catalog—and when you live in this kind of place, you have also the obligation to invent your gods. And my god was the written word. In the beginning was the word, and in the end was redemption. If it's heavy handed, it's heavy handed. I was a heavy-hearted fool, falling in and out of the pages I was writing and reading, the world blurring in and out of focus.

Irving, John. *A Prayer for Owen Meany*. New York: Ballantine, 1989.

———. *The World According to Garp*. New York: Ballantine, 1989.

It would take three years for the world to come into focus, but when it did, I was living an entirely different story (more or less), and in a different place. In this story, I am a husband, having married right out of college. In this story, I have a bachelor's degree in English. In this story, my wife's name is Kelli and we have moved from our college town in southern Utah to another college town in northern Utah. The town is called Logan and was equidistant between our two families (mine was two hours north across the Idaho border, hers was two hours south of Logan, near Salt Lake). We arrived jobless and unloaded our belongings into a mouse-infested apartment behind a grocery store. We were living on what little graduation and wedding money we had received, but put most of that toward our deposit and first month's rent. We ate nothing but rice and potatoes. Kelli did stints as a substitute teacher and applied around the valley for various jobs, but the phone never rang. Her brother-in-law was a car salesman who, from time to time, would hire Kelli to help him set up car shows at dealerships around the region. The money was sporadic, but when it came in, it was good.

My office in our apartment was high-ceilinged with dirty, powder-blue walls, red carpet, and one tall window that looked into our backyard. It was a small space—taller than it was wide or deep and without a closet. Just four walls, a door, and the window with its white muslin of a curtain yellowed by time and neglect. But it was enough, for the time being. I had one cheap particleboard bookcase with the fake wood grain, the same mass-produced crappy bookcase college students cart home from Ultra-Mega-Mart, and a few planks of pine with cinder blocks. Together, they held my small library. I hung a corkboard on the wall and posted witticisms and zingers about the writing life and notices for submissions and contests. I decorated my office with clippings from magazines, photos of Fitzgerald at his desk and Hemingway on safari. My computer—ancient by today's standard—crowded my writing desk, the centerpiece of my office.

In the evenings, we invited friends over—friends who had also moved from southern Utah to northern Utah to find jobs or be close to family. We cooked in our grimy kitchen and played board games and drank cheap liquor. And when we didn't have friends over, Kelli and I would watch television and I would get drunk and pass out on the couch.

In the mornings, under the aching fog of perpetual hangovers, I would write. I was working on a bad novel which pulled me through the sharp, brittle light of day, what with the rhythmic machinations of discipline if nothing else. The writing I produced was awful, but the action of writing was invaluable. It was like rehearsing for a career I dreamed to have one day. This was our routine, more or less, for several months. After the New Year I blew our last twenty-dollar bill on *Writers' Market 1999*. Kelli was angry and had reason to be. Our bills were overdue. Our cupboards were empty. And there seemed to be no safe haven awaiting us anytime in the future. "If I'm going to write," I argued, "I need to know where to send my work."

For three days we didn't talk.

And so the mornings blew by. Outside the snows came and our heating bills soared while mice scratched around in our closets. I drank discount coffee and wrote bad fiction. I surfed writing sites on our dial-up Internet connection. I leafed through the *Writers' Market*—the contents of which, I was beginning to realize, were all online (an irksome fact I decided not to share with Kelli). And I began to read. Haunted by the fear that I had pissed away my one chance to prove myself in college, I started making a list of books to consume.

In my journal, I scribbled the following lines: "I have recently completed the book *Nine Stories* by Salinger and have re-read *One Hundred Years of Solitude* by Marquez. Currently reading 4 simultaneously: *Junky* (Burroughs); *Disuniting of America* (Schlesinger); re-reading *Essays* (Emerson); and *Desert Solitaire*."

The journal entry is embarrassingly self-conscious, strained, overly earnest, and makes no apologies about its brandy-swilling, beret-wearing, smoking-jacket, riding-boots, scarf-donning, faux-intellectual posture. "Following these works," I snooted, "I will be taking up other works in order to educate myself. From my library [which consisted of a whopping thirty or so books] I shall select these as viable readings for my re-education:

The Damned Human Race, Twain
Animal Farm, Orwell
Heart of Darkness, Conrad
Who Will Tell the People, Greider
The Last Days of Socrates, Plato (*The Republic*)
Crime and Punishment, Dostoevsky
Richard III, Shakespeare
Up from Slavery, Washington
Cannery Row, Steinbeck
Asimov on Astronomy, Asimov
Made in America, Bryson

I had a head full of ideas. Kelli had a head full of worries. And we slogged on through the days, phoning home to borrow money. A hundred bucks here. Two hundred there. Four hundred to get us through the month. Each call a verdict on our—no, *my*—apparent failure to make it in this world, for my ultimate failures as a man. We would argue like so many young and anxious couples whose marriage begins to fatigue under the weight of financial strain. "You need to get a job, Brandon," Kelli would say.

"I'm trying."

"Not hard enough. And you know something else?"

"What?"

"You might have to lower your standards a little."

At this, I would throw a temper tantrum. "We have degrees! It's not supposed to be like this!" It was a foolish, naïve line of thinking, I knew, but I felt it needed to be said. The first-generation college student is supposed to do well! Bootstraps and the American dream and all that shit. This was a common rant.

"We just graduated, Brandon. You have to give it time."

My wife—the consummate voice of reason.

I'd throw my hands in the air and disappear into my office, slamming the door behind me. Me—the consummate door slammer. The bone-headed gesture worked as a piece of punctuation following any argument. (Sometimes, though, you find yourself with a hollow-core door, light on the hinges. When you try to slam these doors, a fiendish pocket of air acts as a buffer, so try all you like, throw your entire body into the gesture, but the hollow-cores are unslammable, which, in turn, makes those prone to door-slamming want to slam the unslammables all the more, but I digress). Afterward, another cold front of silence would drift into our drafty apartment, and its cool air stood between us for hours, then days, until one of us broke and apologized. And that person was usually and rightfully me.

The days mounted. I mailed off resumes, interviewed at various companies and programs around the valley. A librarian job. Director of a civic club. Coordinator of a literacy project. Manager of a big-box restaurant. A technical writer. And each time, I got the same response: thanks, but no thanks.

I slipped lower and lower. Unemployment, I wrote in my journal, is "ruining me." "I feel lost." And so one afternoon while Kelli was in Salt Lake City working at a car show, I pawned a stack of CDs and bought a membership at the only full-service bar in town. (In Utah, real bars don't exist. Private clubs do. And you have to sport a membership to drink in these clubs). I called a friend and had him meet me there. His story wasn't all that different than mine. He too was recently married. He was also unemployed and he and his wife lived with her parents outside of town. I smoked cigarettes and drank whiskies and felt my body lift a little.

"We need to go into business," I had said. Or maybe he said it, but we both agreed.

"There's money to be made in this valley."

"Loads of money, man."

"It's just finding that *one* thing."

"Yeah. That one fucking thing."

He stayed only about an hour and then tottered out the door into the afternoon light. I remained parked on the barstool until I spent the last of my money. On the way home, I wrote a bad check for a twelve-pack of beer and lugged it back to the apartment. When Kelli walked through the door I was passed out on the couch like I always was.

Car shows were becoming more of a regular gig, and as a result, Kelli was gone more often. I moped around the house unshowered, unshaven, and spent unreasonable amounts of time watching Food Network. (Tip: when you're unemployed and living on rice and potatoes, it's not a great idea to spend hours per day watching gourmet cooking shows. It leads one to write more bad checks for saffron and wild duck and truffle oil and midshelf wine.) I don't know how it happened, but I had slipped into the world of the deadbeat guy. I downed bags of chips. Cracked the first beer in the afternoon, sometimes earlier. Beer in hand, I would scratch myself, and slap my gut, which was growing at an astonishing rate.

Classy.

Kelli would come home from a car show, exhausted and spent, having been on the road all day. She would pull the day's earnings from her purse and look around the filthy apartment and its sink full of dishes, and her drunken, layabout husband dusted in chip crumbs on the couch. "How was your day?" She would ask.

I would shrug.

Soon a fight would erupt.

Entries from my journal at the time: "I drink too much, especially as of late." "I'm gaining more weight, especially lately." "Today I am sloth. Yesterday too. And tomorrow will be here in a few moments and I will be sloth then as well." Some entries were angry. "I'm fucking lost. Twenty-six years old and I can't find a job worth the time I spent preparing."

When she wasn't on the road traveling to car dealerships or substitute teaching, Kelli sent out more resumes and cover letters. And one day, it all paid off. She was offered a full-time position managing a temp agency. Benefits, a salary, car allowance, and a cell phone. The job saved us. "I can't believe I got it!" she shouted. We did a dance in the living room. We drew back the curtains and let the light flood our run-down apartment. We spent what little money we had on dinner that night and did another dance in the kitchen.

Meanwhile, I had shaved, showered, and cleaned the house. Most important, I swallowed my pride and applied for the one job I knew I could get. But it was a miserable situation. Desperate and empty-handed, I went back to work at Monarch Marketing in the northern Utah office. It was the same bloated, globalized corporate mega-dynamo it had always been. But even though I had been in middle-management all through college, I had to start off on the phones, the bottom rung. Worse still, I was dumped in the worst department in the entire company: collections—for The Big Cell Phone Company. It worked like this: if you had a cell phone with this company and didn't pay your bill, the company would deactivate your service, and the next time you tried to call someone—your lover or mother or friend, say—you were automatically rerouted to the collections department, to someone like me. Worse yet, The Big Cell Phone Company's billing system didn't work. So honest, bill-paying people (people unlike me, for example) would send their payment in on time, but their remittances wouldn't post for thirty, sixty, even up to ninety days, and these poor people were continually re-routed to our department. For eight hours a day, I was screamed at. "You asshole," they would shriek. "You belong in jail!"

Part of me believed them.

Day in and day out, I would stand in front of my monitor and stare out over the sedate, white fluorescent lighting and the un-ending sea of blue cubicles and wonder how in the hell I had got-ten there. A bank of cubicles at the north end of the calling floor monitored every billable second. They called themselves "Mission Control," a name I found laughable. They had to account for ev-ery second of call time, and, most important, every second that someone in the fluorescent hive wasn't on the phones. If you had to piss, for instance, you raised your hand, flagged down a floor supervisor, and filled out an "Exception Form"—which document-ed (1) Why you were off the phone; (2) Whether or not your ab-sence was (A) Work Related or (B) Personal; and (3) The ap-proximate amount of time you expected to be, in this instance, in the bathroom. The floor supervisor would then file the Excep-tion Form with Mission Control, and on their go-ahead (which they didn't always grant), you got the all-clear to use the toilet. But to use the toilet, you had to log off the computer, unplug your headset, gather your personal items (magazines, books, pen-cils, forms, doodads, gizmos, etc.) and take it all with you. Mean-while, the floor traffic director, whose sole job entailed placing warm butts in empty chairs, directed someone else to take your seat, thereby minimizing the time your station stood idle. After you drag your jumble of shit into the bathroom and do your busi-ness, you have to file back in line and wait for the floor traffic di-rector to find an empty seat for you to warm.

This is called Efficiency.

To insulate myself from this absurdity, I read books. In be-tween calls. During breaks. During lunch. I read constantly. Save the throng of Mormon employees who read their scriptures in their cubicles while crocheting, I was one of the few workers who brought books to work.

And so under the flat-white corporate lights, I stole away into the pages of a book the way my younger, more boyish self stole away into the sheets of a stranger's bed.

It's funny how the world can catch up with you, or how you can catch up with the world. We hadn't lived in Logan long before I ran into Milo, the curly haired Ayn Rand/Hemingway fan I got on with in Cedar City. He, too, had moved to Logan (as had Spenser, my fraternity brother). He was attending Utah State University as a theater major and had written a couple of plays that had won regional awards and competitions. "Let's start a writers' group," I said, or he said. And we did. Because we lived in Cache County, we would call it, cleverly, or not so cleverly, the Cache-22. We met biweekly and drank a lot and work-shopped our stories. On board were Jeff and Sarah. Hilarious, sharp, generous, and self-effacing, Jeff was a writer whose leanings tilted toward science fiction. And Sarah, Jeff's wife, was a theater instructor at USU. She was from England and was charming and brilliant in equal measure. Erica, whose angular body seemed (to me) sexually charged, was an actress and writer. Then it was Milo and me. A solid group. And part of the group's dynamics demanded that we swap books. The first on the list was *A Prayer for Owen Meany*. They had all read it, had gushed about it time and again, and because I was the odd man out, it became incumbent on me to read the volume. At the time, I hadn't even heard of John Irving, but once I picked up APOM, I started to understand—first in flickers—then in one narrative rush—the source of my group's adoration.

I fell for the book like a hapless lover. I became its student, devotee, a proselytizer, and promoter. I showed it to Spenser. You have to read it! You just have to read it! But what, I wonder, lay at the root of its psychic appeal for me? It is, by and large, a book of youth. And from *The Mad Scientist's Club* to Huck Finn, *Rock 'n' Roll Nights*, or *The Outsiders*, this coming-of-age theme, this tint of the bildungsroman, was hugely attractive to me (per-haps because I always saw myself as coming of age: never having fully come of age, but always in the process, midway, mid-arc, in medias res). That might have been part of it, indeed, a significant part. But beyond that, there is something else, I think. Something sad, perhaps. Something elusive. Perhaps because I have always veered into the swamps and bogs of melodrama, the meadows of the Romantic, and into the portals of the past; perhaps because I have always felt that I had been born in the wrong place and at the wrong time, and into the wrong name—perhaps that is why I gulped down these pages. Here was a story set in New Hampshire. Here was a family (the Wheelwrights) of propriety, of old money. Here I could see words like *Headmaster* and *Academy* trotted out into the text as naturally as days fall in a week. Strangely, wrongly, perhaps, I was less interested in Owen Meany—the small "chosen" boy with a BIG VOICE whose working-class family I recognized—than I was in the narrator's world. "Above all things that she despised," the narrator, John Wheelwright, tells us, "what my grandmother loathed most was lack of effort; this struck Dan Needham [John's stepfather] as a peculiar hatred, because Harriet Wheelwright had never worked a day in her life—nor had she ever expected my mother to work; and she never once assigned me a single chore."

Maybe because I have been something of a closet Victorian all my days, that is why I was so struck by this book. And not just the story, but the roomy prose, the calisthenics on the page. All of it, the whole package, led me by the hand into an indulgent daydream of the east where I imagined myself wealthy and proper. I couldn't see at the time, however, just how empty this kind of daydream is, how misguided. Owen Meany was the (tragic) hero of the book. Not John Wheelwright. I couldn't see the virtue in being a small boy with a BIG VOICE from a scrape-together family. I could only see the perceived virtues of being a well-to-do boy with a monied voice and a stiff-collar background. You read what you want into some books, and I was reading in the wrong direction. But influence is a powerful thing.

Meanwhile, life at Monarch Marketing was unbearable. Mandatory overtime. Corporate lunacy. Meaningless paperwork collated by mindless drones. All the old metaphors applied. The cogs. The machine. The belly of the beast. And all for a low, low seven dollars an hour! I'd had enough.

The kicker, though, came on Christmas morning—our first Christmas in Logan, our first Christmas as a married couple. I was scheduled to work ten hours: 6:00 a.m. to 4:00 p.m. No choice in the matter. You work your forced, fucked-in-the-ass overtime, or you get fired. Period. So off to work I went. As I drove the dreaded route, snow blew through the dark and across the roads. Holiday lights winked here and there. Not a car out save the line of them turning left into Monarch's parking lot. And there's me, in my car with some crappy Christmas song on the radio, banging my fist on my frozen dash, and screaming: "FUUUUUUUUUUUUUUUUUUUUUUCK!"

Inside, I swiped my ID badge and stood in line and waited for the floor director to find me an empty seat. Every time a manager walked by, I'd give him the stink-eye, like, *"That's right MOTHERFUCKER. I'm looking at you! Bring it!"*

I lasted two hours, if that. Then I stood, put my computer on idle, left my headset and badge in my cubicle, and left.

"Do you have an Exception Form?" My manager said, clomping toward me with his clipboard.

"I don't need one, Brian."

"It's company policy that if you're going to be off the phones . . ."

"I don't work here anymore. Merry Christmas."

And that was that.

What I wanted to say, what the fictional Brandon would have said is, "Go fuck yourself, Brian, you fucking cake-eater," and then I would have kicked down his cubicle and brained him with a laser printer. But that was the fictional Brandon. The real Brandon just left quietly.

I was home and jobless, once again, by breakfast.

To her credit, Kelli was understanding, or at least as understanding as one can be under the circumstances. The job made me miserable, and when I was miserable, we were both miserable. "Something will turn up," she said. I nodded and we turned our attentions to what was a very spare and but nice holiday.

As luck would have it, something did turn up. I got a job at an environmental consulting firm as their office manager. It was my job to run payroll, taxes, accounts payable and receivable, insurance, everything. When they offered me the gig, I hesitated, and said, "You know I was an English major in college, right?" Meaning not a business major.

"We do things a little differently around here."

I was evidently a risk they were willing to take, even after what must have been a disastrous training session. I'd ask questions like "Which ones are the receivables, and which are the payables?" Or "Is an invoice the same thing as a receipt?" Or "What [the fuck] is a spreadsheet?"

Soon, however, I got my head around it, more or less. Occasionally, I got to do fieldwork like water sampling or vegetation surveys. A small firm, the company employed, at peak times (usually during the summer field season), something on the order of fourteen to fifteen people. We had an in-house water lab, a macroinvertebrate lab, riverboats, camping gear, a map room, a conference room, a library, and lots of offices. Our biggest clients tended to be government agencies like the Department of Environmental Quality (DEQ), the Division of Wildlife Resources (DWR), or other entities like the Bureau of Indian Affairs. My boss, a garrulous limnologist, served as an expert witness in a number of state and federal trials where water rights—one of the most hotly contested issues beyond the hundredth meridian—were front and center. He was one of the leading experts on Bear Lake—one of the cleanest inland lakes in the United States. Compared to Monarch, this small shop was a place of respite. We kept beer in one of the laboratory fridges, and you could pretty much come and go as you pleased.

On slow afternoons, we would sit around the office or in the lab, or out in the garage and shoot the shit and sip on our beers and tell stories. Sometimes, though, when a project deadline was bearing down, we all stayed late to get done what needed getting done. It wasn't forced, fucked-in-the-ass overtime. It was something we wanted to do, something we were a part of. It was, I imagined, a chapter torn from the pages of Steinbeck's *Cannery Row* and our company was Doc Ricketts's lab. Once again, I was mistaking my real life for the lives in books.

My starting pay wasn't great, but it wasn't bad either, and quickly I earned several raises over a short period of time. Between the two of us, Kelli and I soon were making enough money to leave the rat-infested apartment and buy a small house. We closed on the deal, got the keys on our first-year anniversary, as it turned out, and ate fast-food on the bare and empty floor. I had an upstairs office with wooden floors and built-in bookshelves. By all outward appearances, it looked as if we had landed smack dab in the American Dream.

And what's the American Dream without your wife coming to you on a rainy afternoon in your small home wearing a big smile and bearing the gift of a baby rattle? But because you're slow, you don't quite get why she is giving you a baby rattle, but then it hits, and holy shit, you're going to be a father, boy, whether you are ready or not! And so you have a good job and you're reading your books and you've got this little house with a small fence and a small green yard and big trees and blue sky all around, and in nine months your life will change dramatically. You will have to become a man once and for all.

I beamed, my head rocketing through the clouds. Giddy beyond giddy.

Kelli's pregnancy wasn't as smooth as we had hoped for, however. At an appointment, we learn that Kelli has preeclampsia. "It's like high blood pressure," the doctor tells us. "And it can affect both you and the baby."

My heart goes wonky in my chest, my body cold and wooden. "But it will be OK, right?"

Kelli is the strong one here, back straight, inquisitive. While my questions tend toward the abstract, hers are calculated. She wants numbers, specifics, as if she has come prepared for this report.

It's a fairly common condition, the doctor tells us, and as long as we monitor it, everything should be fine. There can be cases, however, when it is more serious. When I ask, "Like how serious?" the doctor tells us that it can be like death-serious.

I nearly vomit right there on his feet.

The doctor puts Kelli on bed rest. We're a month out, and she is not, under any circumstances, to do anything. Meanwhile, I have been frantic to clean the house and fetch her meals and drinks and extra pillows and movies and books and magazines and CDs and peanut butter and ointment and icepacks and toenail clippers and dust cloths and pencils and scissors for coupon-clipping and notepads for lists of things she needs, and everything else. The constant bustle keeps me busy and that is what I need, what we both need. Even though I am not the praying type, I find myself issuing crazy, desperate, wacky prayers to gods unknown. For my wife. For my child whose heart beats inside this woman.

Mason Fitzgerald Schrand (named after F. Scott) was born without incident in the small hours of September 11, 2000. I remember cutting the umbilical cord (which I hadn't expected to do). I remember weighing him. I remember wanting to sleep. I also took pains to remember the data because that seemed like an important thing to do. His weight, length, time of birth. Memorizing the data seemed like good father behavior, and I wanted to start out right. I wanted to do the stand-up thing.

In those early days of fatherhood, when I wasn't reading *What to Expect the First Year*, I was reading John Irving's *The World According to Garp*. For all its quirky, frightening, and hilarious moments, for all the high jinks and romp, *Garp* laid bare in full, unapologetic terms all my insecurities not only as a wannabe writer but also as a wannabe father. It was alarming, for instance, just how easily I could recognize elements of myself in Garp. And it wasn't just that like me, Garp too had been a wrestler or that he liked to write, but it was his panicked and bumbling attempts at fatherhood, his fever-pitched paranoia that the world, as Irving put it, was simply too dangerous for children. When Garp ran after and cursed at the cars that sped through his neighborhood, for instance, I felt the sheer inevitability of disaster not just in his life but in my own. Our home abutted the property of the local high school, and daily a league of pimply hotheads gunned their junkers down our street. I would stand on my lawn and watch in jaw-set anger as they roasted their tires in front of my house, forcing me to tuck Mason's head in my jacket while the foul black cloud of rubber smoke swirled around us. "Sons-a-bitches," I'd mutter.

Once every couple of weeks during Mason's infancy, I would reconvene our writing group and inflict upon them bad fiction, fiction that started to smack of John Irving. I am unsure of the extent to which his influence was evident in the writing I submitted to our group. If it was evident, they were gentle enough to withhold comparison, or at least directly. I had "finished" what I referred to as my "first book": "The Thunderground: A Waltz Through Barbed Wire." For four years, I had written and distributed an underground newspaper (read: an 8½ × 11 sheet of randomly disseminated vitriol), and this volume was a lashing together of those issues with commentary on each issue and the circumstances that "inspired" it. It was a strange narrative. Fiction and nonfiction slapped together willy-nilly. In a sense, it was an account of my undergraduate delirium (that's the nonfiction part) seen through the eyes of my protagonist, Horkpod Penelope Rajeem (the fictional part), a sassy, smart college student and writer of searing prose who drove a 1974 Gremlin and who spent her nights clickety-clacking away on a motormouth of a typewriter. And by "finished" I mean I had hit the 100-or-so page mark and felt satisfied that Horkpod had thrown her Smith Corona into the back of her '74 Gremlin and gunned it into the sunset. She had stirred up some campus controversy and was thrilled by the shit storm she had concocted. But she also knew it was time to move on: "Cocoons had been popped," I wrote. "Forbidden fruit had been devoured. Aleister Crowley did the rumba with Virgil . . . A farmer's melons swelled. Ozzy Osbourne ate a whole fried chicken. A slinky took the elevator. Boys went sterile. Girls ran for convents. And Horkpod Penelope Rajeem felt her panties moisten. It was time to leave." Etcetera, etcetera. Fortunately (for everyone), I drawered the sucker and started punching away on another book titled "Untime Returning"—a novel. I peeled chapters out of the project and fed them to the Cache-22 group. It was a muddled text that was suffocating under the centuries-old press of influence. It was a clogged narrative of aimless prose. For the most part, the result was a lot of hangovers. The novel centered on a central character, Maria (my second female protagonist), who was returning to her hometown—a town not unlike Soda Springs, Idaho—where she aimed to reconcile a dark secret lurking in her past, blah, blah, blah. But like my other attempts at writing, "Untime Returning" was terrible. It was too much Irving, too much Ondaatje, too much Dinesen, and not enough me. The one thing it did have going for it, though, was that it was set in the West, in Idaho. And the setting and landscape—all sagebrush and basalt flows—was central to my conception of what the novel might become. I wasn't turning my back on my rural Idaho roots. I was seeing those roots and that hardscrabble place as somehow important, necessary, and urgent for the first time. Urgent because I had this child in my life, and if I looked down the dark hallway of lineage, down that vast corridor of time and history, and did the math, then I would come to realize that the baby in the bassinette is a sixth-generation westerner. There's something to that, I thought, and it was something I would try to articulate in my story.

Kittredge, William. *Hole in the Sky.* New York: Vintage, 1992.

Three months after Mason was born, I started the long and frightening process of applying to graduate school. Kelli and I had discussed it at length. "Now that we have a family," we'd say, letting the gravity of that word—family—sink in, it was time to get serious about our future. Applying to graduate school is a tedious and daunting process for people who have sterling undergraduate transcripts and who *get* college, let alone those who spent seven years earning an underwhelming 2.175 GPA. A lot of busywork goes into the application process. You have to write a letter of intent, for instance. You've got to get letters of recommendation. This step in the process isn't a big deal unless you are forced to ask (read: beg) the professors who watched you fail out of their classes time and again. Then it complicates things. You have also to take the entrance exams like the GRE. But I suck at taking exams, especially long exams. My mind stays focused for about the first hour and then I start checking out the girl in the next row, or I start daydreaming or doodling, and then, as time begins to run out, I just start filling in circles at random—C, C, C, D, A, B, B, C—thinking I've got to get *some* of them right just on the law of probability. Beyond a short attention span, though, I'm just not that smart when it comes to standardized-test questions, especially the kind that look something like this:

David and Deborah each have 12 purple light bulbs for their lighting board. Alex, who lives downstairs, and who has been boning Deborah on the side, has 4 green light bulbs for the same lighting board. Ron, who lives at 5th and Maple St., has just been shit-canned from Office Max and has only 6 yellow light bulbs. Alice, who has been sleeping with David, doesn't like light bulbs, preferring coconuts instead, of which she owns 46. If Ron breaks 2 of his light bulbs, how many pancakes will Alex make on Tuesday morning after humping Deborah?

Some people, the smart ones, just breeze through these questions while I sweat and draw diagrams of light bulbs and coconuts and pancakes, all the while pulling my hair out.

So I didn't have exams on my side either.

Eventually, I pulled it all together and submitted the application, for better or worse, to Utah State University. Every day after work, I would come home, give Mason a bottle, and check the mail and phone messages. For weeks, I heard nothing. And for weeks, I drank myself to sleep. Finally, after a month of hand-wringing, my worst fears were confirmed: my application had been denied. Shocker, there. "We regret to inform you," the letter said. No need to read further than that. Ironically, the only promising part of my application was my entrance exam. But the rest was a wreck. I didn't even fully understand which program I was applying to. To wit:

IV. PLEASE SELECT THE PROGRAM TRACK YOU WOULD LIKE
TO PURSUE:
A.) Literary Studies
B.) American Studies

Which did I want to pursue as my graduate track? The nonexistent C option: American literary studies. But apparently I had skipped this question and somewhere else in the application I had penciled in my invented track ("We're a bit confused," they would later write, "about your intent.") My abysmal grades, iffy letters of recommendation, murky letter of intent, and my noodly paper on Edmund Spenser's *The Faerie Queene* all amounted to an apologetic nay. Sort of. "Take some upper-division courses," they said, "and we might reevaluate your application." Here was a glimmer, a backdoor in. I was by turns dejected and hopeful, and so I would hoist a drink nightly to the gloom and hope in equal measure.

That spring, I enrolled in two classes and quickly became the embarrassing nontraditional, nonmatriculated student with too much to lose and too much to prove in every class, oblivious to his own one-upmanship. My arm ached from raising it all too often: "Call on me! I know the answer!" (But what, really, did I know? I was a closet metal-head from the rural sticks of southern Idaho.) And yet my arm stretched toward the ceiling as if my life depended on answering every question correctly. Here was my chance to make up for the tepidity of my high school and undergraduate days. Here was my chance to reorder some things, to get my act together, to be on my best behavior rather than reverting to my old ways of misbehavior. Becoming a graduate student would also mean I would become a good father and good husband, or so I reasoned.

After that first term, they admitted me and tossed in a teaching assistant gig. Rewards for the bald-faced overachiever. I was thrilled. I was gathering books like they were stars to be gathered from the twilight, each one a road sign, a point of light on some vast cartography of fate: read this book, learn how to live. In addition to working part-time at the environmental consulting firm, I was in my first semester of a master's program and teaching my first class—freshman composition—and could not have been happier, buried as I was in work.

Part of that work involved reading William Kittredge's *Hole in the Sky*. Reading Kittredge was like having earth-old secrets revealed to you. Reading Kittredge was a message in a bottle flung to shore. Reading Kittredge was like breathing for the first time, was like seeing words you knew existed but couldn't access all lined up on the page in such a way as to say this is what you have been looking for all your long misspent days. Kittredge, who had grown up in the western social class of the "propertied," had one boot in the world of Oregon's vast Warner Valley and the other in the dreamscape of books and ideas. His divided attentions, split loyalties, and silent betrayals, created in him something he called craziness. He was crazy with ideas. Crazy with sex, always wanting to get laid. And he was crazy with drink. But mostly he was crazy with trying to write his way out of a master narrative that had been prescribed for him. Like Kittredge, I, too, had grown up in a rural backwater. His Warner Valley was recognizable. It was a sagebrush swath of land inhabited with people I knew as well as I knew my own skies and blood. And his family could have been my own in many ways. The bone deep recognition, though, came about differently. Certain passages cut right through me. "And there began one of the retreats of my life," he writes, "which I have to respect as a move, however neurotic, toward salvation. As illiterate boys will, I came to books, and learned to value ideas beyond anything actual."

There is in his words an enduring ache, and it was an ache I had carried around for so long. The ache of illiterate boys—of those who seem fated for misbehavior—can be the most haunting, most damaging, reckless, feckless, consuming, tender, and loveliest aches of all. I had been born into this feral tribe of illiterate boys who had gone mad on books and ideas. When everything—literature, the world, the cosmos—goes to the head of the illiterate boy, we cannot be surprised by his sudden craziness, by the savage lunacy that threatens to undo him. How then, and by what means, is he to reach that far shore of safety? How then, and by what means, can the boy rewrite the prescribed narrative given him? When redemption comes, will he recognize it? Can he intuit that the very books that unravel him are the books that will rescue him from the sagebrush valley of madness?

Oh, the madness, it comes.

What drives you mad is the split nature of your person, your duplicitous ways, your utter capacity for paradox. On the one hand, the father in me took seriously my new station as a graduate student. I was teaching freshman composition and reading truckloads of books. I was doing well in my seminars and had, for the first time in my life, the grades to show for it. On the other hand, I found a crowd of beer-drinking grad students in whose company I could unleash the boy within me. We would pass every Friday at a bar downtown. It seemed like a grad-student thing to do. We met for lunch and left two or three hours later, drunk and chatty. Then it became five hours later. Then we took both lunch and dinner at the bar. Afterward, I would stagger home stupid-drunk and broke, pulling crumpled bar receipts from my pockets. I would stumble into the nursery and sway over the crib with a big dumb smile on my face.

Another unsavory, yet representative, tidbit from those days of duplicity: one night after another long bender at the bar, I wake to take a leak but never make it to the bathroom. Instead, I mistake the bed for the toilet, and piss all over the covers and the hardwood floor. The next morning, Kelli shakes me. "We need to talk," she said.

My head was pounding, my stomach sick. "About what?" I croaked in the milky light.

"You don't remember anything about last night, do you?"

"Remember what?"

"I had to change the bedding in the middle of the night because you were too drunk to find the bathroom, that's what."

A pause. One of those long pauses, a shadow of silence, the dark waters of regret and misgiving pooling between us.

I sit up in bed and put my hand to my head.

"I can't live like this," she says from the doorway. She leans into the frame as if she no longer has the strength to stand or the pride to pretend she can. Then: "I have to go work."

She leaves with Mason in the car seat.

I lie back in bed throwing my numb gaze to the ceiling, and exhale.

One event in a series of like events, a pattern as old as river stone and the water that carves it. At a party a few weeks later, I fell down a friend's staircase, ripping the handrail out of the wall on my way down. The next day another friend stops by the house. He is tall and dark. Attends a dojo, has a pit bull, and studies weaponry and Vietnam but is gentle and sincere. He's the kind of guy who checks in on his friends. Who drives them home from the bars, who loans them money. I am nursing a hangover. He chuckles, and shakes his head. "You broke Miranda's handrail. Do you remember that?"

I shake my head. "Is she pissed?"

"No," he says. "She laughed. Said it was broken to begin with."

"Still."

"Yeah. Still."

Another pause. A different kind. This is the friend pause. A world away from the spouse pause. I hang my head.

He stands, stretches. "I've got papers to grade. You all right?"

I nod.

During the semesters when my teaching schedule included Fridays, I would frequently call my officemate from the bar to cancel class. "Hey, man," I'd say. "Can you walk over to my class and tell them I am home with a sick baby?"

He would agree to do it, and I'd say, "Thanks, man! You're the best!"

Give a man a half a chance and count the ways in which he'll shoot it down.

Soon, Kelli grows tired of my marathon binge drinking, and, with Mason in tow, she starts to spend the weekends at her mother's house, two hours south. Who could blame her? We hadn't been married three years, and already she was taking time away from me.

One evening, just as I'm leaving a friend's house after several drinks, I grab a beer from his fridge and head for the door. One for the road, if you will. Because my car is in the shop that week, I am borrowing a work truck, a big, long-bedded, king-cab thing with a camper shell. I clamber in, set the unopened beer on the seat, fire up the engine, and switch on the lights. That's when I see the cop car drive by slowly. Casually, I stow the beer under the seat and pull from the curb. That's when he whips around and hits his lights. The red and blue lights flood the quiet neighborhood.

I try to think how many drinks I've had while my pulse races, and my hands begin shaking. If I get another DUI, I'm fucked. There isn't any other way around it. If I get another DUI, I will lose my wife, my child, grad school, everything. In the rear-view, I can see the cop throwing his mag-light beam into the camper-shell window on his long, slow walk to question me. I reach across the bench seat and fidget with the glove box until it opens. I grab the sheaf of paperwork that he will ask for. My hands won't stop shaking and then the mag-light beam falls on my face, searches the cabin of the truck. I'm terrified that the beer beneath the seat is visible, has rolled forward, has revealed the real story here.

I roll my window down, palms wet with sweat.

"Evening," he says.

I nod. "Anything wrong?" I say, careful not to breathe directly on him.

"Well, I ran your plate and the number didn't match the vehicle, but I see that I was off on one letter." The license plate, I knew, had a ding on the letter O making it look like an D.

"It's my boss's truck. I'm just borrowing it."

He motions toward the paperwork. I hand it to him, along with my license. The paperwork rattles with the shaking of my hand. Damp with sweat.

He scans it with his flashlight, and without looking up, he says, "You haven't been drinking or anything like that, have you?"

Tricky question. In the span of maybe one to two seconds, I find my answer: "Actually, I had a beer with a friend at dinner."

"I thought I could smell it."

"I figured you could."

He looks at me and holds his finger up. "I want you to follow my finger. Just your eyes." He sweeps it left, then right, then toward the middle, then back right again."

My knees begin to quiver and I rub my palm against my jeans. My heart pounds in concussive thuds.

He puts his finger down, hands me my paperwork and license. "Where are you going?"

"Home."

"Where's home?"

"Second south. By the high school."

"I want you to go straight there. Got it?"

"Yes, sir." I nearly start crying right then and there. I start the truck and pull out toward home, making all kinds of vows in my head. Always making vows, this guy.

When, oh when, will the boy learn?

And yet.

And yet, I pulled a 4.0 every semester (except my first when I got an A-). And yet my teaching evaluations were great (frequently canceled Friday classes played no small role in those evals, I'm sure.) And yet, my professors were sending me to conferences and throwing opportunity after opportunity to me, bones to the bloodhound, they threw them. And at work, I continued to get raises and run the business. Never underestimate the power of paradox, the undertow of madness. Nothing is easy. Everything is complicated. Kittredge taught me as much. "I had been taught to pay attention to my own contradictory instructions," he says.

"Like most of us I'd learned to tell myself to be this and be that, to be both the one thing and the other, to be loved and to be honest, to be sexy and get laid all the time and yet to be desired and true and also anything you want because it's nobody's business but your own, betray them all and know they'll understand deep in their hearts because they are betraying you. Be one and everything at the same time. Until you are nothing."

Until you are soaring sick and mad, the illiterate boy set loose in the world, misbehaving his way into miseries he can't name.

In ways I couldn't articulate at the time, Kittredge became truer to me than John Irving or Dinesen or Ondaatje. If not truer, then more necessary. If I had been misreading my way into basement miseries, then *Hole in the Sky* was a book that enabled me, I think, to read my way into familiar terrain, into country I recognized. There was, I think, a slow realization that I need not be of New Hampshire stock, that I need not attend an academy with a headmaster in order to live a meaningful life. Kittredge reminded me that the way out of the prescribed narrative was to write my own, and that my own began with the ground beneath my feet. Finding that ground was one way to safeguard myself from the madness. But it was also Kittredge who said that you can survive the duplicity and the madness, that the illiterate boy can become a man. And that, I think, mattered most of all.

Lopez, Barry. *About This Life*. New York: Vintage, 1998.

Before Kittredge there was Barry Lopez. He visited Utah State University during that first semester when I was the nonmatriculated student. I hadn't yet established myself as anything but another face haunting the hallways of Ray B. West, the building at Utah State that housed the English department. So my behavior during that semester swung wildly and unpredictably from silence to endless yammering, from monkish absorption to show-off. In short, I couldn't read the culture of graduate studies. How do graduate students behave, after all? How do they dress? And, most notably, what language do they speak? Theirs was, indeed, a foreign language to me. I learned all kinds of words that semester. Words I hadn't really considered before. Words like imperialist, epistemology, codify, and other, operative words words I knew but hadn't dispatched in quite the way graduate students did: negotiate, reify, unpack, and deconstruct. Graduate students, I soon learned, were always "looking at" things. They were also "concerned" about things. And what they were looking at and concerned with always related to their theses. At receptions and gatherings, graduate students chatted about their theses while spearing plattered hunks of salmon with toothpicks. "I'm looking at colonial captivity narratives such as Mary Rowlandson's as a way to unpack and negotiate contested gender spaces within colonial patriarchal familial/theocratic structures," one might say over a glass of chardonnay. "Primarily, I am concerned with the usurpation of voice in the codified systems of rhetorical/gendered/ social milieus during the Second Great Awakening." And then they would ask me what I was "looking at," and I would have to tell them I had no idea. "Something about the West, I think," I'd say. Then I would chug my wine and mosey away into a safer place.

But if I was uncomfortable, I was also in love. I was drop-your-heart-on-the-ground in love with this world. I made the walk up the long staircase that led to campus, my nose buried in my book, glancing up only occasionally to avoid tripping or when a hot girl walked by. I read in the early morning before Mason woke. I read at night after he went to sleep. I read on our front lawn on the weekends. I filled legal pads with hundreds of notes on the texts I was reading, and then I would staple the set of notes together and fold them into their respective volumes. Sometimes, I would type out my notes. I bought a filing cabinet and started collecting articles, sources, and other material that might serve me one day. I carried a small notebook with me into which I scribbled all the new words I bumped into. At night in my study, I would look them up in my brand-new Oxford English Dictionary (the one I bought late one night while drinking single malt scotch and surfing the Internet. The next morning I woke with a hangover and the head-slapping realization that I had ordered a three-hundred-dollar compact dictionary without consulting my wife. Needless to say, the purchase didn't go over well. It was an old story: me buying books with our last dab of money). And in class, I would trot those newly acquired words out into the discussion as if they had been mine all along, as if I had been born into such a language, as if my verbal prowess had been hard-wired into my genetic map, as if I had attended an academy with a headmaster. It was a newer version of me. Part lie. Part hunger. Part beauty.

Because Lopez was visiting that semester, we had been assigned his exquisite collection of essays, *About This Life: Journeys on the Threshold of Memory*. I am not the type to lob a word like *exquisite* out there any old time, but it belongs solidly to this book. Because it *is* exquisite. It is, I think, near perfect, as collections go. Of course I had never heard of Barry Lopez prior to that semester. Here was a writer who seemed to fall between John Irving and Hemingway. Someone who had both eastern and western roots. Someone who cared about stories and place and the natural world but also someone who grew up in a way that secret parts of me envied. And those secret parts of me burned green with envy when I read certain passages of Lopez. Talking of his move from rural California to Manhattan, he writes, "I thrived in the city in spite of the change in landscapes. I focused on my studies—Latin, history, English literature, French, art (a class taught be the painter John Sloan's widow)—a standard Jesuit regimen, light in the sciences. I developed into a fast, strong athlete, and graduated with letters in three varsity sports and a scholastic average high enough to have gained me entry to almost any university."

Lucky bastard! I recall thinking when I read such lines. Some of my less-than-forgiving peers cried *arrogance!* when we discussed the book, or at least the essays we had been assigned. So while some—not all, mind you—of my peers fumed, I envied.

So in class, I came to his defense. "He is not without concession," I argued. And then I cited the rest of that passage because it fortified my argument (always go to the text; a lesson I was learning quickly), but also because I recognized what he had to say. I saw an adumbration of myself in his concession. It was like seeing the faint gray image of yourself floating and then breaking on rippled water. "I felt privileged rather than deserving of all this," he continues. "I understood that my Jesuit education, my social and economic class, my good grades. . . my white skin, my hegemony of my religion all pointed toward being well received in the world. In my private heart, though, thinking back to the years in California and forgetting those early days of privilege . . . I felt dressed in borrowed clothes. How did I come to be here?"

I could—and did—begin to ask that same question of myself.

In-class disagreements on the Lopez material ceased when the living, breathing man walked into our classroom, a small seminar room with a long table. He was stylishly dressed and wore a khaki cap.

What ensued after twenty or so minutes of discussion was a question of story and its value. While I don't recall specifically how we arrived at the following question, I will take to the grave its outcome. Lopez turned to me and said, "What is the shortest story you have ever read?"

I thought for a minute, and then answered, "A Very Short Story," by Hemingway.

"And did you like it?"

Yes, I did like it. But I couldn't get the words out. I didn't know if I should say yes, or no, or I don't know, or maybe, or what do YOU THINK, or what. So I froze. All the doors in my mind slammed shut. An ice age set in. Synapses no longer fired. My blood stopped flowing. My heart turned to plastic. Everyone stared at me. My professor looked at me, and then she intensified her look. Still nothing.

Lopez tried to help out. "I mean, as far as stories go, did you enjoy it? As a story?"

And still, nothing. Someone started to snicker. A few whispers escaped. The only reaction my body produced was to expel a rivulet of sweat down my forehead. The most I got out of my mouth was a staccato line of, "I . . . I . . . I . . ."

A minute passed.

And then two.

A dog aged seven years.

Baseball season started and ended.

Finally the man cut me loose. "Okay," he said, breaking the tension. "I don't want you to feel like I'm setting you up or anything, but I would say that is a good story."

I hung my head. My shoulders rolled forward and my ears burned red. What was said during the rest of the period, I do not know. I wanted to bolt and never return. Or: I wanted to stop the conversation and set the record straight: I wasn't an idiot (or at least not in the answering-a-question-in-the-class-room-sense), really. I was capable of answering a simple question. But I was too consumed with acting like a graduate student, with speaking the right language, with wearing the right, borrowed clothes, that I had lost myself when it came to the simplest of responses. What I wanted to say is what Milo would have said: "Fan-fucking-tastic story!" What I wanted to say is that I thought it was a small work of genius. That it was infinitely harder to write a short story—as Mark Twain has reminded us—than it was to write a long one. That is what I wanted to say. But my mind and newly acquired graduate student identity ambushed me. I thought it through too much. I was aware of how those in feminist studies viewed Hemingway, and perhaps rightly so. I was aware that he was yet another dead white guy, etc. etc. So, on the one hand, if I told the truth, would I risk short-sightedness, self-awareness, critical acumen? But if I lied and said no as a way of safeguarding myself from those kinds of criticisms (i.e., that Hemingway was a misogynist), what would that make me? So in the end, I did the worst thing. I said nothing.

Later the same day, but in a different class, I had the opportunity to make a fool of myself once more. I was in a 400-level senior capstone course. All undergrads and me, the interloper, the old, married guy. Lopez's book was tacked on to the syllabus part way into the semester, and although I would later read the entire book, would in fact, reread it again, circling back to particular essays over and over (e.g., "Flight" and "The Whaleboat"), I hadn't read it all the way through in time for Lopez's visit.

During the hour or so visit, Lopez talked about the duties of the writer and the seriousness of the writer's station in life. It was, he said, a profession of great obligation. Everything he said, I drank in, star-struck grad student as I was. At the end of the hour, I asked him to sign my copy of ATL. He agreed, and as he was autographing the page, he asked me where I was from.

"Soda Springs, Idaho," I said. "Have you ever heard of it?"

He looked at me for a second and then said, clicked his pen, and said, "Well, yeah."

"Cool," I said. And then I thanked him, and ducked out.

Fast forward two weeks. I am on the couch at home reading the rest of ATL when I come to the essay, "Replacing Memory." It is a spring day, the sun bright outside my window. Kelli is at work and Mason is taking a nap. The sunlight warms the living room in a way that makes you drowsy, that makes you grateful for being alive. It is the kind of afternoon light that asks you to stretch. Everything is right in the world. I am a father, husband, eager-beaver wannabe graduate student, reader, wannabe writer, homeowner, and all-around American. Then I hit section III in the essay, and I spit cola through my nose. Subtitled, "Bear River, Idaho, 1991," the section opens a stone's throw from Soda Springs, Idaho. *Ever heard of it? Well, yeah.* The closer I read the essay, the more I begin to realize that he had driven right by my town in 1991, may have even driven through it. The year I graduated from high school. While I was likely lying on my back at KBRV/KFIS reading Emerson's "Self Reliance," or, alternately, trying to unclasp some girl's unclaspable bra, Barry Lopez, a man I wouldn't know about or whose words I wouldn't read for another ten years, was passing through my extended backyard. Maybe you could write about rural Idaho, I thought, and maybe people would actually read it.

Menand, Louis. *The Metaphysical Club: The Story of Ideas in America*. New York: Farrar, Straus, and Giroux, 2002.

In the spring of 2003, I finished my MA in American Studies at Utah State University. Shortly before graduation, I learned that I had been accepted into the MFA program in creative writing at the University of Idaho, which is located way up in the wooded panhandle. This time around the application process was different. This time I knew what I wanted to do. I had the letters, and a decent writing sample. This time I didn't have to enter graduate school through the back entrance. This time it was legit. They gave me a teaching assistant gig, some scholarship money, and Kelli and I said, "Well, that's that. We're going."

Although I am a fifth-generation Idahoan, I had never been to Moscow (pronounced Moss-Coe)—a funky, woodsy college town on the Palouse, a place of rolling hills and forest. So I was ecstatic.

I was ecstatic in part because I also wanted to get into some remote swath of wooded land and write. I was smart enough to see it as a Romantic notion, some Thoreauvian daydream, but I didn't care.

But there were other reasons to be ecstatic, too. Kelli and I both saw the move as a second chance for us, for our family, and so her enthusiasm bloomed too. We knew exactly the kind of place we wanted. An older home outside of town. A wood-burning stove. Quick access to the mountains. A garden space. Put another way, we needed time and distance. I needed to recast my focus. We needed a do-over. A CTRL-Z on the past five years.

Soon, I swapped my nights at the bar for nights in my office surfing the Internet for the kind of house we wanted. And then one night I found one. It was a large two-story Victorian home in Troy—a tiny logging town eleven miles east of Moscow. It had a terraced yard, an apple tree, room for a garden, wood-burning stove, and a wide front porch that overlooked the town. Plus it was cheap. But there was a hitch: we had to take it immediately. This meant a deposit and first month's rent on top of our current mortgage payment.

The added hitch was that Kelli needed to find a job in Moscow.

If we had endured our share of incongruous times in Utah, and indeed we did, it seemed that those times were over. Call it providence. Call it coincidence. Call it dumb luck. But at the very time we needed to decide on the house, an excellent job at the University of Idaho fell from the sky and right into Kelli's hands. Better yet, it was a job in the dean's office of my college, which meant we would share much of the same social circle.

But there was hitch there, as well. She had to start at once. This was late May 2003. I had to stay in Utah for the summer and sell our house while she and Mason moved—with all our belongings—into unknown country. Two months and hundreds of miles separated us. At night, I would walk around our empty home listening to the haunting echoes of my footfalls on hardwood, and I started to imagine in gut-rending detail what life might look like or feel like without Kelli, without Mason, and I would panic.

Other things caused me to panic while I was alone in that house, certain realities: becoming a writer, for instance, is a crackpot notion. Something best left to madmen who are single, skinny, and who smoke a lot. Sane people don't prod their family into the woods so they can become a writer. Who was it that said, "I'm going to the woods with a typewriter and a gun, and it's going to be one or the other"? It was best to stay with my Thoreauvian daydream to keep me from rooting around in parts of my head where logic took up residence and issued forth reprimands, reproaches, and recriminations. Logic said that it would be easier to become a pilot, surgeon, or astronaut than it would be a writer. Logic said that I had a family to think about. Logic said just getting one thing published would be next to impossible, let alone a book or many books. Fool's gold, pie in the sky, pipe dreams, the lot of it. Better to get a job and settle down. Then if the fancy strikes, sharpen the pencil and amuse yourself with the stories you'd like to tell. Just don't make your family suffer while you chase rainbows. That's what logic said.

But the daydream arrives at night like a lover. Like a drug. Like hypnosis. Before you know it, you're afloat in its crystal waters and you can see yourself. Yes, you can see yourself writing in a little studio in a grove of trees and throwing hunks of wood on the fire that fuels your wonder. Yes, best to stay with the daydream.

At summer's end, I joined them. I turned over the empty house to a realtor friend and packed my camping mattress, sleeping bag, radio, books, and a few other incidentals into my boxy Land Cruiser. I couldn't get to Idaho fast enough. I checked the map and clocked my route. The drive, I knew, would not be easy. In all, it would take between eleven and twelve hours. Once I crossed the Utah border, I had all of Idaho to traverse, mostly by highway. There exists no freeway that connects the panhandle with the rest of the state. In order to travel to Moscow, you either have to light out northwest on I-84 toward Boise and then cut north along a winding highway for another five to six hours. Or, you can bear northeast on I-15, cross into Montana, veer northwest toward Missoula, taking I-90 to the top of Montana, and hook due west into the Idaho panhandle, and then drive *south* for another two hours.

After consulting the map, I chose the Missoula route. Much of that route would be on the interstate, so at least it would appear as if I were getting there faster. So after what was a long and hot August drive, I arrived, red-eyed—sweaty heap. Troy, population seven hundred, huddled in a wooded gorge and was lined with steep streets, smelled of rip-sawed lumber, and you could hear the continual whine of the mill working day and night. At one edge of town, decks of logs rose up from the mill yard, and at the other grain elevators towered over Main Street.

When I lurched my Land Cruiser into the driveway, Kelli and Mason rushed out to greet me. It was a sweet reunion. (Is that sentimental? If so, fine. We were short on sentimentality in those days). That night we cooked a fabulous dinner and drank a bottle of red wine and I played with Mason until he sacked out on the couch.

In September, I ordered two cords of tamarack and spent much of those warm afternoons splitting and stacking wood. I learned how to handle an axe, how to split kindling, how to avoid knots, and how to adjust the draft in the stove. We canned tomatoes and green beans and Kelli made bread and I would play with Mason on our spacious living room floor. I wrote in the mornings to the hiss and pop of the stove. In the evenings, I prepared for class. We were alone, which is another way of saying we were together for the first time since Mason was born.

The town had everything we needed all within two blocks. A general market where you could buy a few groceries and household items like candles or fuses or pencils. You could buy wine, fishing tackle, rent movies, and try your luck on lottery tickets. We had a library, post office, city hall, barber, mechanic, three bars, and a liquor store. On the edge of town, between the mill and the city park, you could find a gas-station with a laundry, and the White Pine Cafe. Behind our house, a gravel road meandered into a grove scored by a brambly gulch and I would take morning walks through there after writing.

Of course not all of them were sunshine days, plucked from the hypnotic pages of some Wordsworthian poem. Chopping wood wasn't always a bucolic pastime, for instance. Funny how the Romantic notions of a writer's idyll can wither and deflate under the cruelties of the real world. There is nothing Romantic, for instance, about coming home after work in January to an icebox of a house having to split kindling outside in the dark and light a fire while your wife and son hop from one foot to another to keep the blood flowing, their breath clouding the air in whitish plumes. There is nothing Romantic, for instance, about the constant burns on your fingers, hands, and wrists from all those quick, fiery flesh-on-stove kisses, which is much more frequent than you could ever have imagined. Nor is there anything Romantic about living with splinters on a daily basis.

Consider, too, our snake problem. The landlord omitted the part about the snake colonies that resided in the stony terraces of our yard. We're not talking rattlers or boas or cobras, just your average garter snake. But to me, a snake is a snake is a snake, and I squeal like a little kid every time I see one. My neighbors—some of them third- and fourth-generation loggers—must have rolled their eyes and clucked their tongues whenever they spied me bolting from a snake. On any given afternoon while tending my garden or splitting wood, I would see one in my periphery or one would slide by my boot, and I would squawk and fling whatever tool I had in hand—hatchet, hammer, hoe—and high-step it to the porch. Meanwhile, the neighbor kid—a redheaded seven-year-old boy with wide-set eyes who always ran around in his dirty white underwear—would swing snakes over his head like a rodeo man and fling them one by one into the street or onto the roof of his house while I watched from my porch goggle-eyed in abject paralysis. Once, I broached the snake situation with a different neighbor who just laughed: "Wait 'til you hit one with the lawnmower." Jesus! I thought. I hadn't considered that! And so began a paradox. When the grass is long, you can't see the snakes sliding through its blades (and I'd rather be able to spot them at a distance than be surprised). But I was petrified of hitting one with a mower and my mind would obsess over the sliding-*thunk!* sound it would make and the spangles of blood and snake-meat on my trousers and on and on.

Egad.

One can go crazy with such thoughts, and such thoughts can be tamped down by distractions, by routines. It was our routine, for instance, that I would pull Mason in his wagon to the post office, where I would mail essays to magazines and pick up rejection slips. I would then pull him to the market for an ice cream cone and then on to the park, where I would read the mail and watch him play. Or I would chase him across the baseball diamond and we would crash in the outfield. There was no epiphany in those days. No lightning strike, no sudden moment of clarity. But there was the slow and inevitable accumulation of days beneath the sky and the rhythms of activity you might call life.

Later that same year. It's late in the evening and several of us young, eager, furtively competitive graduate students are gathered on couches in the Garden Lounge, one of the local bars in Moscow, a favorite haunt of the writer-types. It's a smoky college place with high ceilings and attractive waitresses who wear glitter on their eyelids. It is situated in an old brick hotel—the Moscow Hotel (a place later converted into apartments), and because of the brick and the bar and the hotel, I am constantly reminded of home, of Soda Springs and our family-run bar, hotel, and café, and for this reason alone, I tend to prefer the Garden Lounge over the other bars in town. But it is on this particular night that I am talking with a professor of mine who mentions *The Metaphysical Club* and when I return my blank expression meaning that I have not read, in fact haven't even heard of it (the ongoing story of my life), he balks: "But you got your master's in American Studies, right?"

I sip from my martini and nod apologetically. There is a shrug in my shoulders that is supposed to communicate something akin to, "Yeah, well, you know: so many books, so little time." But the more he talks, the more I become fascinated but not for the same reasons he is interested in the book. I come to see the book not just as a rumination on the development of ideas and pragmatism in American life (a point my professor had articulated along the way), but as a foundational text to help me situate my ongoing obsession with Captain John Codman, a

Bostonian ship captain who had summered in Soda Springs at the turn of the century.

It's a mammoth book with a scope to match its heft. Here was Oliver Wendell Holmes (who had gone to school with Codman at the Andover Academy). Here was Louis Agasiz (with whom the Codmans visited on their ten-month stay in Brazil). Here was Pierce (whom Codman's wife knew very well.) In short, here was a book that filled in the blanks, that fleshed out the narrative, a book that brought life to the era in which this long-lost mariner had lived.

As it turned out, I was doing well that semester and had ample reason to be eager, to be thrilled. Not just with being in a MFA Program and studying with great teachers and students. Not just with living in a woodsy town with a warm home heated by the wood I split. Not just with the manic ritual of writing and sending off half-baked essays and picking up one-sentence rejection letters. And not just because I was finally present, more or less, as a father and husband. But because I had carved out a sliver of success for myself. My first semester in the program, I had seen my first essay come to light in a decent journal. I had won a contest before I left Utah State, published an essay review in a scholarly journal, and had won another essay contest on the West. Plus, my workshops were going well, for the most part, or at least as well as any MFA workshop can go. Scant praise interlaced with having your ass handed to you on a weekly basis. Then a week or so before my conversation in the Garden Lounge, I had won a grant that would allow me to travel to Boston to work in the Codman archives.

My plan was epic. Because Codman had traveled from Boston to the West and back via train when the railroad was peaking (circa 1872—or three years after the Transcontinental Railroad was completed, the final spike having been driven, however awkwardly, at Promontory, Utah), I would retrace his steps 132 years later, when the passenger railroad industry was tumbling and on life-support. The red-faced truth of the matter was that

I was terrified of flying, especially that far. The quirky historical connection I was trying to draw was a cover story for the truth.

In all, I would spend six days on the train. Three there, and three back. And the one book I took, committed to read, was *The Metaphysical Club*. Because of its breadth and heft and subject matter (heady stuff, man!), I figured it would take the entire round trip. But as my train chugged into the Back Bay Station in Boston, I had sprinted past the final page and was diving into the back matter, notating the notes, filling my notebooks if not my head with connections big and small, quirky facts, incidents, minutia. The whole world (or at least that of the nineteenth and early twentieth century) had opened up before me. I got Menand's larger points about the fundamental development of American philosophy by the by, but it was such a peripheral point that it scarcely mattered.

At the train station, I was to meet Katherine, a friend from college, from my falling down days in southern Utah, who had taken a marketing job in Boston. She shared an apartment in Arlington with three or four girls of her Mormon persuasion and had offered me a couch. Generous beyond generous, considering I would be there for close to two weeks.

As a professional graduate student, I had come to prefer the utility of backpacks over the bulkiness of luggage, so when I dragged my gigantic North Face backpack into the train station, a tall, elegant Middle Eastern man sized me up, and said, "Are you looking for the youth hostel?"

I let my backpack slide to the floor, and managed an exhausted, "No."

"Oh," he said and smiled. "You just looked lost, that is all."

Was it that obvious, I wondered? Was it obvious that this barnyard boy had been loosed into the genteel avenues and promenades of John Irving? Was it obvious that I was terrified and hugely out of place? Did panic or bewilderment or nausea burn in my eyes? Had I tracked my western cow-shit into the East already? To what degree did I stick out? In every degree imaginable, I presume.

My first course of action involved scouting out a pay phone, that once-vital relic of a world that has slipped into antiquity. Here was another reason I stood out: I didn't have a cell phone. I hadn't really had a need for one and they felt, well, too showy, too glitzy for a guy who swung an axe in the Idaho woods. And so I had taken a kind of strange pride in not having one. But because I had arrived late and because I didn't have any quarters, I began to see the inherent usefulness of cell phones and wished to God I had one at the time. What salvation! What comfort! Everyone I saw gripped those slick little suckers like their last lifelines. Everyone, that is, except for me. Soon, I began to wonder, sweat, and worry that I would never make it out of the train station.

Finally, I saw Katherine waving her arms and that champion, contagious smile I knew so well in college. She was a wide-eyed wonder with hair the color of a smoldering fire. I have never had a thing for redheads in general, but I very often entertained a benign crush on Katherine. She was safe. She was devout Mormon and a close friend of Kelli's, but I know a lot of guys in college who were taken with her. When I spotted her, she made a dash open-armed and gave me a big gathering hug. Though her breasts smashed squarely against me, it was a friend-safe, butt-out hug. I was self-conscious through the entire ten second episode because I must have smelled like my seventh-grade locker room. Three days on the rails doesn't do much for a guy's hygiene, much less his looks.

Joining Katherine at the train station was her friend Tiffany. She was what you might call oh-my-god hot. But she was, I would later learn, a more devout Mormon than Katherine (not that Katherine wasn't devout). She was also distant and cold. She was wealthy, that much was clear (she was Old Money + Mormon persuasion + Harvard student = a Mitt Romney Mormon). The train station wilted her demeanor despite her half-hearted and shallow attempts at pleasantries. You could see that she felt dirty there, that she wanted to phone daddy at once. And in less than two minutes, it became easy to hate her. I would say the feeling was probably mutual but that would presume that I was worth enough of her attention to incite an emotion as demanding as hate, which something told me I wasn't. I felt like just a strange and unfortunate creature in her midst, an unsightly nuisance. A momentary agitation in her days of monied tranquility. . And so to pass the short amount of time I spent with her was to live in crushing defeat. Boys from the sagebrush country are vulnerable and foolish in ways you might not expect.

But if Tiffany was rich and cold, then Katherine's roommates were sights for humbled eyes. Or at least they put on their game faces. Each of them was from Utah, transplants in the East, making their way in Beantown. And each of them—like Katherine, like Tiffany—was devout, with one exception. One roommate, who I will call Jamie, was tall, blonde, and tan and wore eye-popping short skirts and low jeans. Her hips and long legs made my insides whir like pinwheels. Added bonus: she was a singer. I learned this about halfway through my stay. I had been in the Codman archives all day, sleuthing through boxes and letters, making notes and copies, and then had retired to the pub I had adopted as my after-hours haunt. On this night I had something like three martinis when I caught the subway to Arlington. She let me in, and it was just the two of us in the house. She had been out with a guy. I had been out by myself. She was, it seemed, a bit tipsy, but I couldn't be sure. I, on the other hand, was happy-drunk. We chatted like magpies about Utah and growing up in a Mormon culture when you didn't really buy into their faith, etc. I was on one couch and she was on the other with her legs crossed. Everyone once in a while, she would uncross them and part her thighs ever so slightly so I could see the hint of light blue panties. Then after I got my glimpse, my eyefix, she would pin her knees together, closing off the dark wonders that existed in her skirt. Then, leaning forward, her full breasts parked over her knees, she asked me a favor: "Can I sing to you?"

The apartment was silent. Just two strangers in a room on a Wednesday night in Arlington. Outside, a dog barked in the darkness. A low rush of street traffic sang its song. Sirens bellowed out there where the halogens glowed their false twilight. And in this flat, the two of us. Me with my heart knocking like a hammer at a locked door, and Jamie leaning toward me with a bashful, pink-lipped smile. "Is that weird? If I sing to you?"

"*No*," I almost shouted. "I mean, it's cool. Totally cool, you know. Like, totally."

"It's just that I have had this song in my head all night. I wrote it this morning, and I have been dying to sing it to someone."

"Sing away," I said and crossed my legs.

And sing she did. My god! How she sang! To this day, I can't recall if she was great or terrible or something in between, but I was leveled, smitten, stuck on her legs and her voice and her dark mystery. Then she strolled upstairs, taking her time, catlike, swinging her hips, looking back once at me to coo, "'Night," and hooked a lock of blonde hair behind her ear. God, Boston was great!

Boston was great, as it happened. Sometimes *too* great. I passed my days deep in archivery, waist deep in the flotsam of history. Even on the first day it became frightfully clear that I was on to something huge, something much bigger than what I secretly suspected I was capable of rendering into any meaningful narrative. If it is the scholar's curse to have precious few sources, the twin curse is to have too many. After the first week, I had been flooded. But I was high on my work. I felt legitimate and hard working in all the significant ivory tower ways. I was hunting down a lost legend, I was doing what my professors called "primary research," and I was living out some sliver of my Victorian daydream.

Inconsistent with that Victorian vision, however, was my misbehavior. On another evening, after a full eight-hour day of eye-straining reading, photocopying, sniffing, poking, and digging, I had gone to Davis Square, where I got some dinner and one too many martinis. Boozy, I stumbled back to the flat, let myself in, and hit the bathroom to take a piss. Oh, the joy of relieving the bladder! The release, the powerhouse rush of relief! Except one thing. One thing I should have pieced together. I should have noticed that the bathroom door was shut before I entered. I should have, but didn't, notice the steam in the room. The closed shower curtain. The running water. So there I am, swaying over the toilet, urinating at full power when I hear a girl's voice: "Um, I'm not quite *done*!" Penis in hand, I throw a quick glance over my shoulder, and she is peeking out from the behind curtain, dark, soaking hair. My eyes goggle to the size of pie tins.

"Doh!" I bark. And: "Er, sorry!" And: "One second!" All the while, I'm trying to tie it off and zip it up, only to whiz on my pants and shoes. "Son-of-a . . . !"

The girl is not Katherine. Nor is it the singer. It's a different roommate, one of the quiet and serious ones. I'm close enough that my elbow could touch the curtain. She's close enough that I can *feel* her lathery nakedness like a heat wave burning a hole of embarrassment through both of our souls. But mostly mine. I bolt out the door, nearly slamming it behind me, and retire to the couch and the darkness with a pillow over my head, over my shame.

The next morning was, thank god, my last day in Boston. I wanted to leave and never come back. The dread of the shower mishap was too much to bear. The humiliation, the red-faced embarrassment, the sudden awkwardness as heavy and thick as weather. I wanted to go home. To my wife. To my son. To a better version of myself.

Back home, I cover my small office floor in notes and photocopies of articles written by John Codman. I create a rough draft chronology of his life and travels and pin it to my wall. I discover a small press devoted to reprinting classic equestrian books, particularly those involving long rides. Turns out, the small press had stumbled upon one of John Codman's books—*Winter Sketch-*

es from the Saddle (1888)—and were set to reprint it. On a lark, I e-mailed them and offered to write an introduction. They jumped at the chance, and so the eager beaver graduate student went to work on writing an introduction to John Codman's book. Menand's hefty volume played no small part in teaching me the history of the late nineteenth century.

When summer began to ebb and the students moved back to Moscow for the fall semester, when the rolling hills of the Palouse had turned from green to a harvest brass, a bunch of us gathered once again at the Garden Lounge. It was there in that old brick building that I ran into the professor who recommended *The Metaphysical Club.* We yammered on about this part of the book and that part of the book while the rest of the crowd (most of whom had been *assigned* the book in his class) steered clear of the conversation.

From almost anywhere in the Garden Lounge you can see a giant sign that hangs high on the brick wall: HOTEL. As we talked about the virtues and luminosity of Menand's book, I would sip from my drink and look up at the sign now and then. HOTEL. HOTEL. HOTEL.

I knew something about growing up in a hotel. So with the Codman introduction and Boston behind me, I had now to settle on a thesis topic, and the idea of my upbringing in an old brick hotel, café, and bar kept washing to shore.

And just like that, the idea that had been lapping at my feet found its purchase, and soon I was tracking down not the diaphanous image of an old ship captain, but the ghost of my childhood self tramping about in an old hotel. It seemed that all my literary roads headed south, into the sagebrush of my youth.

Morrison, Jim. *Wilderness: The Lost Writings of Jim Morrison.* Vol. 1. New York: Vintage, 1988.

For the rest of junior high and some of high school, I stayed true to my imitation of an Outsider from S. E. Hinton's book. It was an identity that suited me, one that lent itself to an extension of that identity: I had become a rocker, not unlike Gary Specter in Strasser's *Rock 'n' Roll Nights*. But soon I started to see the sad and empty limitations of this rocker daydream—itself a brand of fiction—and could, much to my dismay, discern where the guitar distortion ended and I began. Music would remain important, but my tastes and wandering interests shifted. And while I cannot pinpoint exactly when I started to shelve my Metallica albums in preference to the cosmic, circus organ vibes of The Doors, I think it was sometime during my senior year of high school. At night in my room, I would write embarrassing poetry by candle light while Morrison crooned from my stereo about how no one would get out of here alive. *This shit is deep*, I remember thinking. I would pick up the phone and call this girl Polly who was also into The Doors. She had dark skin, long dark hair, emerald eyes, full lips—a solitaire of a hottie on the sagebrush front.

"He was so *misunderstood*, you know?" I would say into the phone.

And she would agree. "Their songs are like so *deep*."

"I *know!*"

So when I learned that Morrison wrote "poetry," that there were books out there filled with his "lost writings," I couldn't help myself. I hitched a ride to the nearest book-

store (Pocatello, 108 miles round-trip) and bought three volumes. I read nearly all of them on the way home, mesmerized
over lines like, "Midnight/criminal metabolism of guilt forest/
Rattlesnakes whistles castanets." I had *no idea* what this meant
(still don't), but that was okay. Poetry wasn't written to be understood. This was clear to me. After all, I reasoned, if his poetry was easily understood then it would forestall the possibility
of his being *misunderstood*, and if he wasn't misunderstood, then
he wouldn't be an artist. And I wouldn't have made the two-hour
journey to fetch his poems.

Soon it became urgent that I *read* Morrison to Polly (the urgency here stemming from her oh-my-god good looks) late at
night on the phone while my candle threw billowing shapes over
my walls. And when that wouldn't do, I would pump my bicycle
across town beneath our three traffic lights (which are turned
to blinking mode at 10:00 p.m.), and rap at her door, breathless. She would step out on the stoop. The porch light would
snap on, and I would wave Morrison in her face. "Check it out!"
I would say.

Little surprise, then, that I started smoking pot in college.
And dropping acid and writing even worse and more embarrassing poetry. Wedged between my mustardy suit with the puffy
shoulders phase and my polo-shirt-wearing frat-boy phase was
my short-lived hippie-stoner phase. I had a Jim Morrison poster
on my dorm-room wall, which is another way of saying I was the
early nineties kid who was imitating the sixties kid who was imitating Jim Morrison. I wore beaded necklaces. I got ironic and
spacey. In my literature courses, I would cite Morrison at every
turn. The lecture might center on Andrew Marvell or John Milton or Sylvia Plath and my hand would shoot up, the beads
around my neck jumping and clicking. "*Totally* reminds me of
Jim Morrison, you know? He's like talking about like the *same*
thing."

On weekends several of us would drop acid and hike around
in Zion National Park (or Zion National Money Mint, to borrow
from Ed Abbey). Or eat a bunch of mushrooms and go throw

Frisbees around the park until we were incapacitated from idiotic giggling. We formed elaborate theories and related them in serious stoner speak. "You fucking KNOW that the guy who created the Smurfs dropped acid, braw." And: "What's up with Scooby snacks? Like, Shaggy and Scooby are so stoned!" And: "Have you ever read a box of Wheat Thins, braw? They like totally say, "Baked not fried!" And then we would roll over howling in laughter, caught in the throes of the stoner's delirium. These are the inane conversations that all stoners have at one point or another (clichés, the lot of them), and soon the whole scene—the Morrison poster, the necklaces, the bong water, the paranoia, the so-and-so's-a-narc, the bad poetry, the patchouli oil, the incense, the glow sticks, and the goddamn drum-circles, all of it—started to wear on me. Not so much that I gave up the doobage, but enough to retreat from that smoky nonsense.

But I didn't retreat far enough, evidently. Because one day you go for a joyride in the Arizona desert with two friends and a little weed and the lambent drone of "Riders on the Storm," and with your heads swimming like three balloons in so much smoke, you find yourself in a heap of trouble. So you cut your hair, lose the beads and the poster, and turn your attentions elsewhere.

Morrison, Toni. *Beloved*. New York: Plume, 1988.
——. *Sula*. New York: Plume, 1987.

TRANSCRIPT FROM SPRING QUARTER, 1998, THE TERM OF MY GRADUATION.

ENGL 252	INTRO TO DRAMA	B+
ENGL 450	THE NOVEL	A
MATH 101	INTERM ALGEBRA	D+
SOC 101	INTRO TO SOCIOLOGY	C
SPAN 301	BASIC SPAN CONVERS	C
	CURRENT GPA	2.43
	CUMULATIVE GPA	2.175

Sometimes the world comes into focus and grabs your attention, and when it does you find another girl standing there. On the beach, near the cool azure water. No, it's not a fiction. It's real.

For years my fraternity had rented houseboats with the Phi Alpha Beta (later nationalized as Alpha Phi) sorority and floated them on Lake Powell, near Page, Arizona. The subject of these trips and the hoo-ha that went on during these legendary outings is a topic for another occasion, but it was at my final Lake Powell trip that I met Kelli—the woman I would eventually marry. She was president of her Alpha Phi chapter, and I was proconsul (vice president) of Sigma Chi. Storybook attraction here. I had just come through the slaughter of my breakup with Mary and had by this point put the pieces back together. Even though I hadn't forgiven myself (never, in fact, would), I was looking to make myself anew. I needed to shake it up some, change the scenery. So I quit my job at Monarch Marketing after five years, cashed out my 401K (dumb move), and bought a computer with the money (an even dumber move).

The Lake Powell trip is always held in May, so it signaled the end of the school year. But for me, it signaled so much more. Several weeks after the trip, after Kelli and I started dating seriously and after school ended, she moved home to work in northern Utah, and I moved, for the first time since 1991 (when I had hauled the trunk of embarrassments into my dorm room), home to Soda Springs. For the summer. I was going to finish writing "The Thunderground: A Waltz Through Barbed Wire (The Chronicles 1993–1997)."

As it happened, Soda Springs wasn't far from Kaysville, Utah, Kelli's hometown. Only a couple of hours south as the crow flies. So we would meet on weekends and on her days off. During the week, we spent far too much time on the phone, and we wrote letters—long, overwrought, embarrassing letters, but we didn't care. Our heads were over our heels, as they say.

I took a summer job in a 120-year-old general store that my grandmother ran at the edge of a lake. It was the only store in a town of eighteen year-round residents (thirty-five in the summer). One of the only phones in town was a giant yellow rotary unit that hung on the wall in the back of the store. It never rang, and I seldom used it. From there, everywhere was long distance. There was no cell service near the lake. It was precisely what I needed.

Summer campers—typically elderly men and women bedecked in khaki shorts and fanny packs—visited the store in the mornings or afternoons. They bought six-packs of beer, rounds of cheese, and spools of fishing line. They would crack open their beers and we would chat about the level of the lake, the mosquitoes, the trout so-and-so caught, and on and on.

On some afternoons when charcoal thunderheads crowded the horizon, throwing the brushy hills into shadow, and when yellow-headed blackbirds pecked in the gravel parking lot, I would read. I remember rereading Michael Ondaajte's *The Eng-*

lish Patient my first week on the job. And I was rereading Isak Dinesen's *Out of Africa*. I had read both in my modern world literature course but wanted, no, *needed* to read them again, especially OOA. I remember those afternoons with that book. Sitting at the rickety wooden table on the dusty, plankboard floor while summer rain battered the windowpanes and winds tugged at loose sheets of tin roofing, I believed that I was living out some version of her narrative, isolated as I was. I was in the country. I was an outsider among insiders. I was a writer working in a country store. I made imaginative connections between her life and my own, connections, in other words, that didn't really exist.

Out of Africa hit me like a crush, stirring my blood in the same way beautiful women did. I was in the presence of mystery, intelligence, something sapid and beyond my ken. The book was romantic, in a sense, and jibed with that part of me that wanted to live in a different time and in a different place. But beyond the heartbreaking world contained in its pages was the language itself. "I had a farm in Africa, at the foot of the Ngong Hills." These words, weighted and bereft, pulled me in at once. I was struck by her descriptions of the natural world; her command over lyrical prose never risked—at least to me—preciousness. I was struck, too, by the dichotomies between African and Anglo-European societies: "Now, looking back on my life in Africa," she writes, "I feel that it might altogether be described as the existence of a person who had come from a rushed and noisy world, into a still country." As taken as I was by the language, by the story, I was also becoming aware of the complicated role she cast herself in. In class, we had debated whether she was presenting a racist or colonial viewpoint in her text, whether her station of privilege was problematic or arrogant, and whether she was co-opting an entire culture in order to write her book. I couldn't get past that voice, though, thick with money, with culture. I was still a sagebrush boy suffering from a lifetime of cow shit on his shoes, of emerging from his own still country into a rushed and noisy world whose rules I was slowly coming to know through books like *Out of Africa*. The barnyard notion that a boy like me had no business reading a book like that, and the force with which I was smitten with her voice, was a kind of personal anarchy I could get drunk on. Don't let them books go to your head, the barnyarders say. I couldn't let them go to my head fast enough.

And so my summer unfolded, an undulating ribbon of time slowed by words, by stories, and the heart-thrum of long-distance love.

In the fall, Kelli and I met back in Cedar City. She looked at my transcripts, sighed, and, with the click of a ballpoint pen, decided to take over. "We need to get you graduated," she said. She was an A student and I was me. That term she signed me up for 17 credits. The next term, 20 credits; the next, 21; and the summer term—my final in what would amount to seven years in college—11 credits. Instead of getting shitfaced with my friends, I stayed home and studied. Studied like I had never studied before. I even passed all my classes, pulling Bs and Cs in my core classes and high Bs and a couple of As in my English classes. Kelli got me through them. She was, and still is, the master planner, the organizer, the back-on-track guru, the forge-ahead, spearheading, cheerleading advocate I needed.

So it was the final push. And a full load. I was retaking my intro to drama class, hoping to redeem myself. And I was taking it from the same professor. She was also teaching The Novel that semester. Easily one of the most demanding yet rewarding classes of my undergraduate career. The lineup of books was fantastic. Among the list she assigned were Heller's *Catch-22*; Kundera's *The Unbearable Lightness of Being*; Linda Hogan's *Solar Storms*; Beckett's *Molloy*, *Malone Dies*, and *The Unnamable*; and Morrison's *Beloved*.

Beloved, for me, was a puzzle, a riddle to be solved, and its house-of-mirrors complexity helps explain why all of my marginalia terminate with a question mark. It was like reading Faulkner, but not Faulkner. It was like nothing I had read before. I would inhale its pages only to have to stop, regroup, and start again. Morrison's work can be humbling that way, demanding of you a level of thousand-eyes awareness you couldn't fathom before.

And because it was the first book of the quarter, I started out strong. I started out (yet again) to prove myself. That I wasn't a fuck-up. That I wasn't a stoner, a drunk, a fool. The stakes were high. Couldn't have been higher, and I was determined to graduate. Determined to make amends for seven years of drugged-out, drunken, street-stomping lunacy. Ready to evict the boy from the sticks, the barnyarder who boiled to the surface all too often.

This time it was real.

I had a lot going for me that term. In February, I had proposed to Kelli. It was the most heart-engulfing, beautiful, and predictable kind of proposal. But we were young and lustful—our tongues always down each other's throats—and we were in silly, giddy, toe-tickling puppy-dog love, so we thrived on the predictability of the horse-drawn carriage on Valentine's day, and the romantic dinner for two, and the guy on his knee with a ring he bought on borrowed money. Love! Sweet love! Cupid, you sly dog! Firing your arrows into our blazing hearts one by one!

So our days looked like this. Kelli rose at 5:00 a.m. to clean toilets on campus for an extra dab of cash. And I rolled out early to study. In the mornings, I read and tore through my Spanish flash cards and made halfhearted efforts at my sociology homework. In the afternoons I worked out algebra problems on my dry-erase board, and Kelli would correct my mistakes as I scratched my head (*what the fuck is an integer?*). At night I met with a study group for extra tutoring in math. On the weekends, we would paint our futures in bright hues of champagne and success, white picket fences and all the rest. At one point, I had considered enlisting in the Navy and went so far as to pick up some brochures. It seemed like a good idea at the time, warless world that it was. The brochure spelled it all out. Travel the globe! Earn money for college! Become a leader! It seemed exciting, possible, and felt consequential (in a good way).

"At least we would be *stable*," Kelli reasoned. Three days later, the recruiter stopped by my house and delivered the news that the Navy preferred engineering majors over English majors for ocs but that I could still have a great life in the service.

That's when I told him thanks but no thanks.

So we scratched that option off our list and dropped the glossy brochures in the trash. We had also discussed the prospects of my attending graduate school and the ways around my embarrassing transcripts.

This is when anything was possible. On the weekends, we also threw mad, romping parties at Spenser's house. It was Jimmy Buffett all night long and Boat Drinks and good times. If we entered college as boys and girls flung onto the open green of the world, we were then sensing an era coming to a close.

It was also natural to begin applying for jobs. "I need a suit," I had told my mother over the phone. They were still in Las Vegas, in the trailer court behind Boulder Station Casino. "As, like, you know, a graduation gift," I added. And then: "But they are expensive . . . I mean the good ones. And I will be applying for jobs, and all."

"Okay," she said. "You figure about a hundred bucks at least?"

My poor parents.

"Uh, like a lot more," I said.

In the end, they bought me a great suit—the first I ever owned if you don't count the mustardy, puffy shouldered number I bought in Pocatello for a fiver and then shit-canned behind the dorms.

So I had a suit. I was engaged. Poised to graduate (finally). Limitless, cloudless skies awaited! I was doing well in my classes, particularly in the novel class. Sort of. Depends on how you look at the term "doing well." Because it was an afternoon class, Spenser and I were given to bringing in cups of boxed wine to the classroom. Big, cheap, mega-store plastic cups. Forty-ounce industrial-size things. People had to have known that we were drinking in class, what with the swill smelling of paint-stripper and all. And yet we made it a ritual. Twice a week at 2:30 we met at his house for a quick drink, and then we rolled to class, cups in hand, making it there right at 3:30. We had read the material and we were prepared. We were completely invested in the books. Spenser would call me at night. "Dude," he'd say. "What chapter are you on in *Beloved?*"

I was always behind Spenser, the speed-reader.

"Because, *dude*," he'd say with urgency. "Wait until you get to chapter [so and so]. Holy *fuck*, man! It will blow you away." Macho, cocksure frat boys swept up in the folds of beautiful American fiction. *Fuck, man. Fuck!*

Then I would plough through waiting to be blown away and was blown away. The characters. The pacing. The web of history and story and memory rushing forward, leering backward, running headlong into heartache and beauteous doom. Word by word, a song of sorrow strung through the pages of a book that will make you cry and hate and try to mend the broken parts of a past that can't be put back together, no matter how many words or metaphors or books upon books are thrown into it, that empty, gaping well of our collective human past. But you've got Morrison, and so long as you've got Morrison, you've got the closest thing to redemption one can imagine. Redemption for the erasure of time and the memory that goes with it. How she handles time and story through her characters. Time: just one of the few blow-your-frat-boy-mind aspects of the novel.

Success, at least in this class, was right there before me. Even my professor, the intimidating woman whom I wanted to impress all those years, was, well, impressed. "Your engagement in this class has been impressive," she had said at one point toward the end of the term. I beamed, head high, the future a metallic bright.

Then the resume process began. I had it in my mind that the best way to become a writer was to follow the Hemingway model.

Begin at the newspaper. It was a natural transition for me. Between "The Thunderground" and my weekly column for *The University Journal*, I had some newspaper experience. And best of all, I had published a big piece in the *Salt Lake Tribune* a couple of years earlier. It was what I considered to be my first big break. A student photographer at *The University Journal* who had a connection at the *Tribune* rang me up and asked if I could clear the following day to ride to Holden, Utah—a small farming town—to cover the funeral of a local man who had been shot in a friendly-fire accident at Fort Bragg. I leaped, and the two of us—freelancers—drove three hours north, covered the funeral, and I wrote the story in a notebook (in the days before laptops) in the car for the hour and half it took to reach the offices of the *Tribune*. Catching the elevator up to enormous floor of the newsroom, I felt legitimized for the first time in my life. Our contact met us at the elevator and guided us through the maze of cubicles and bustle of people. It was a scene straight out of a movie, a daydream come true. "So," our contact said as we walked, "another struggling Com major?" He was a stocky, suited man with a raspy voice (which I chalked up to smoking), and no small trace of swagger.

"Actually, I'm an English major."

He turned on his heel, sized me up, and grinned. "So you really *can* write!"

I mumbled something self-effacing and looked out across the sea of news-in-progress and to the galaxy of city lights gleaming beyond the office windows.

"I started out as a poet in Boston," he said. "But the news gets in your blood, and, well, here I am." East goes west, West goes east.

He gave me a computer, and I pounded out my piece. We worked out some minor edits here and there, and then I filed the sucker. We got home at just after three in the morning, and I woke feeling like I owned the world. But it wasn't even close to the feeling I got when I bought a copy of the paper that featured my story on the cover of the State page: *"Hero buried among family" by Brandon R. Schrand, special to the Tribune.* And that feeling was topped when I received in my mailbox a check for $125.00. It was the best money I had ever made.

So it never occurred to me NOT to apply for a newspaper gig.

Kelli and I hit the want ads with pens, making lists and pros-and-cons columns, and went to work. She was looking for a managerial job or a position as a museum curator (drawing on her history degree), though those jobs were rare and usually required a master's degree. Soon, I found a job opening at the local paper, *The Daily Spectrum.* It was for a sports writer. That I seldom followed sports at all (much to my shame) didn't deter me. Nor did my ignorance of the basic sports nomenclature (RBI, WAC, PAC 10) prevent me from gussying up my resume and sending it in. Within a few days, the phone rang. I landed an interview thirty minutes south in St. George at the *Spectrum*'s main office. I put on my suit, shaved, slapped cologne on my face, and drove down.

The interview tanked even as it began. The editor asked me some questions about my favorite teams or what I thought of team X in Y series and what did I make of Z player? Or, the standard question, "How about that game last night?" I bullshitted my way through, red-faced, and sweating. Then, when he could see that I was devoid of sports trivia or general knowledge, that I was some wooden dolt sitting before him, he changed tack. "Tell me your life story," he said.

A half-hour later, I had gotten as far as my junior year of high school and how my friends and I used to set off pipe-bombs in the gravel pits.

That is when he cut me off and thanked me for my time. Clearly, my try-to-be-interesting shtick didn't work.

That, and I didn't know shit about sports.

At home, Kelli awaited me, beaming. "How did it go?"

"I think it went okay," I lied.

We were in a holding pattern. Hold your breath.

Seven days before our graduation Kelli had gone home to northern Utah for a bridal shower, and Spenser had thrown an end-of-the-year party and everyone was there. The police showed up as they always did in our small town and told the partygoers to disperse. Boozy and with a head full of big ideas, I decided to engage the police officers, to reason with them, to spin some arguments, to show off a little, to strut my strut. Friends intervened but I wouldn't listen. "That's enough, Schrand," they said. And, "Don't push it, man." But I kept going. At one point, the officers had actually been entertained by my antics and one said, "You might make a good lawyer some day." But when I started poking my finger in his chest citing this and that about the United States Constitution, they tired of my parlor game and cuffed me. "Okay, pal, you're coming with us." They shoved me in the squad car, and while they called off the party, I sat in the back seat with my arms wrenched behind me and cried a drunken cry.

Within the hour, I was sitting in the holding tank in the Iron County jail. I was acting drunk and stupid. "I'm graduating in seven days," I said.

"In what?" One of the officers asked.

"I'm a writer," I said. "A sports writer for the *Daily Spectrum*."

They burst out laughing, taking it as a joke. "Uh-huh," they said. "Brandon Schrand with the *Spectrum*! That's rich."

Everyone was laughing. Such good times. Such, such were the joys!

Not soon enough, my friends bailed me out—("Good night, Brandon Schrand of the *Spectrum*!")—and took me home. The next morning Kelli called. Her voice was like birdsong. I was hung over and wrecked with guilt, so it hurt to listen. The shower was *wonderful*, she said. And the *gifts*! She chimed. *You won't believe gifts we got!*

That is when I told her.

Bless the woman.

That was the downside. The upside said I had a suit for my court appearance. *Looky here! I have a fancy suit, Your Honor, so you know I'm not some scumbag, drop-out, dope-smoking, drunken, barnyard criminal!*

Oh, the court appearance, itself a kind of hangover, a nasty reminder not of who you were on such and such night but of who you are, who you have suddenly become. This is no fiction, the court says. This is real. This is documentary. It is a different kind of narrative, one that doesn't go away. The trouble with criminal histories is they are not read in the past tense. They never purport to explain who a person *was*; they mean to explain who a person *is*. They are read less as static documents recording time-swallowed events and more as clues telegraphing the future. And I was beginning to stack up an impressive history that was threatening to spell out a future story I didn't want to occupy.

A few days after the court rigmarole, I received a letter in my mailbox from *The Daily Spectrum* thanking me for the interview and the interest in their paper, but they had offered the job to someone with more "experience." Best of luck, they said, as they always do, as if it helps soften the punch.

Because I was dumb and because I was mopey and glum over my bout in jail and for not getting the job, I decided to fire off a letter to the guy who had interviewed me. Also, because I was obsessive-compulsive about saving all my mail—good, bad, or otherwise—I made a copy of the letter. I typed it on the Smith Corona motormouth using Southern Utah University letterhead (graduation gift).

18 June 1998

Dear [redacted]:

Sir, I feel curiously compelled to write this missive regarding your paper's ultimate decision to forgo endorsing my employment. Whether I was indeed overqualified or perhaps underqualified [sic], I think it a tragedy that I wasn't even given a chance to prove a thing or two . . . No offense, but news writing is the bottom rung of the writing ladder—I think you know that. News-junkies trudge through years of college to earn degrees that will someday—hopefully—land them a seat in news writing—a medium that targets an 8th grade reading level. Why not stop in Jr. High school [sic]? Why do we need degrees at all? Newswriting [sic] began with the sincerity of a new marriage. But over the years its integrity has eroded, its grace evaporated . . .

With all sincerity, I enjoyed our discussion. I like your style. I find it rather—no, quite—unfortunate that you and me [sic] will not have the opportunity to work together. I had some good jokes to tell.

> Good luck to you and Godspeed.
> Esoterically,
> Brandon R. Schrand, yr locally unemployed writer.

The third time I wore my suit was for graduation. It had been a rough go. Then, finally, on a bright early summer morning it came. The end. Or the beginning, depending on your view. I would take my degree in English Literature, which was another way of saying I was no longer a boy from the sticks clad in small-town clothes and marked by a dialect I couldn't hear. But it was an uneven time. Everything had changed, and in many ways nothing had changed. I was still a restless young man desperate to find his own story, on occasion foolish enough to be hoodwinked by daydreams, by the fictions dazzling on the page. I didn't feel like you should feel upon graduating from college—smart, successful, poised for the world. I felt those things, but I also felt anxious and guilty and low all at once, there in my suit, robe, and cap.

I took one book with me to graduation. It wasn't Morrison. Hers I parked high on my shelf, a pillar among my small collection that began from the titles scribbled on receipts in my Metallica Velcro wallet. The collection had grown some, and hers—like Marquez's or Dinesen's or Hemingway's volumes—spoke back to me and said that I was ahead, somehow, of the rest of the world, even though nothing could have been further from the truth.

The book I took was something closer to home. It was Larry Watson's *Montana 1948*. No one gave it to me. No one recommended it. It was just there, haunting my bookcase. Looking back on it, I wish there was an easy explanation for why I took *Montana 1948* (and not *Crime and Punishment*, say) to my college graduation, but there isn't. It was a shortish book—small enough to pocket—and that may have had something to do with it. But I suspect there was more. Perhaps I was suffering from a bout of nostalgia. Perhaps, in some small way, I wanted to be a boy again in a small rural town, and this book felt like my passage back to antiquity, to Wordsworth's meadows, groves, and streams. Maybe that was it.

Maybe.

All I know is that this story of a twelve-year-old boy growing up in Bentrock, Montana, who existed along that diaphanous line between the world of adults and the one of boys, between the stories in his head on those in real life, was a story I recognized as somehow true and redemptive.

Ondaatje, Michael. *Running in the Family*. New York: Vintage, 1982.

On the inside cover of this book, I have written (as I always do) my name and the year in which I bought it. In this case it reads, "Schrand 2004." But I didn't get around to reading it until 2005, when I was a second-year MFA student who was doing his best to get his shit together as a writer, teacher, student, husband, and father.

I wasn't a completely changed man, of course. Once in awhile, I drank more wine or whisky than I should have. But it wasn't like before. I wasn't down at the bar every night for hours on end, pissing on my shoes in the can. I was with my family having dinner and wine with other families, other writers in the program and their spouses and their children. The dull gray misery inside had given way to something else. The yawping jackal had died like a fire, and the danger at home slipped away like wind in direct proportion, it seemed, to the new swelling in my wife's womb.

Because I was at work on what I imagined to be my first real book, my MFA thesis, a family memoir, I had been told to read *Running in the Family*. It's a beautiful and dangerous story, all honey and vipers, inducing in its reader a frisson of cruel delight. It's a dream on paper, a beam of pleasure that relumes the imagination in hues of wonder. In a word, it's exotic. It's a story you fall into as it falls into you.

But as exotic as its tropical landscape—a landscape that

seems ready to swallow its inhabitants at any moment either by drowning, hungry overgrowth, quicksand, what have you—is also it familiarity in ways that flash around in your mind like a small storm lighting your own memories from the darkly recesses of the past. It is not hyperbole to say that RIF throws a spell on you.

My experience, then, reading the book was schizophrenic. I would read this or that passage about a strange and cultured family (again, a family whose station and old money pedigree I envied) and would be reminded of this or that story from my own life. The triggering effect. The result is that I own a copy of RIF that is filled with bizarre marginalia that have nothing whatever to do with the text itself, the story, this family in the throes of one kind of madness or another, but with the slipshod terrain of my own narrative. The notes are reminders. Flags. Placeholders. Fragments that would lead to the larger story I was trying to piece together about my own odd upbringing in a boomtown hotel. Consider the following jottings:

> Remember to write about driving drunk on w/ Susie on the Ranch Road. We should have died.

A placeholder. A cue card. Yes, I do remember that night, though the scene never found its way into my own family memoir. Gunning my truck down a winding ribbon of gravel road after my high school romance had just collapsed. I had been at a party (the sagebrush nomenclature is a kegger) up in the dark slot of Trail Canyon and decided to leave in a drunken huff. Susie. Yes, Susie. A close friend. The worrier and therapist in the group. She was worried about me. Wanted to talk to me. Wouldn't let me drive but got in the truck anyway. How fast were we going? It's difficult to say. Too fast. I was a drunken, blithering wreck. Susie was screaming at me to slow down. Begging me to stop before we died. Before we sailed off that road into the moonlit fish pond. Before we sailed out of this world forever. Please stop! she shouted. Finally, I did. And she drove us back. Pulled us back from the brink of what lies in the Tragic Heart of Rural America: the young dead.

But that was Idaho. Not Sri Lanka. And it was Ondaatje's father, drunk at the wheel.

Another cue card:

I am a Scavenger.

(To scavenge. Origin?)
Scavenge in the basement for artifacts.
Scavenge for stories.
Scavenge for my story.

Yet, another:

Last night I dreamt that I detonated and destroyed a building I was standing in. The charges thudded two stories below and I could feel them under my feet. Then the whole bldg. went and I went down with it.

What to make of this? Think of the hotel I wanted to write about. Think of that building. Think: how writing about something destroys it. Writing as violence. How you go down with the story you write. Think obvious things, too, like Mason's birthday.

And another:

The Alexander Reservoir.
A full-throated stoppage on the Bear River.
Green and polluted.
What it holds—the sunken bridge, the old railroad, stories,
    secrets.
A gravitational pull—
Anthony drowned.
The rope swing.
And this? Another tragic story of rural America. Another
    story of the young dead.

This is what RIF did to me. Did to my thoughts. My dreams. I would sweat at night. Hair-soaking sweat. My mind was restless because I was reading a restless book and because the book I wanted to write was restless in my imagination. My mind was restless too, because Kelli was pregnant. But that was a good kind of restlessness. I couldn't wait. I wanted another child in my family. One more would make four, which felt more family-like. I was raised an only child which always felt less family-like.

On November 29, 2005, just days before Kelli was due, and sometime after I had finished reading RIF, I wrote in my journal, "Still no girl." We learned her sex and picked the name Madeline Beth; her middle name deriving not from some literary reference, but from my grandmother. A family name. "So we wait in one of the most beautiful snow storms in recent memory. It is late and I've loaded the woodstove up for our nightly fuel."

Two days later, on December 1, 2005, our daughter arrived in the midst of another horrendous Idaho blizzard. (Kelli's scheduled due date was December 7, which, considering Mason's September 11 birthday, would have been too strange to contemplate). I shift my attention from Madeline and Kelli to the blizzard outside and back to them.

Unlike the long and grueling labor Kelli endured with Mason, Madeline's birth was quick and natural. Two hours and it was all over. I cut the umbilical cord and made phone calls. "Well," I told people on the phone, "she was born in a blizzard. You think it might be a sign?"

Winter barrels down on us and snow drifts against our house. We're socked in. I split kindling in the snowy dark and load the stove and try to keep the large house warm. Mason helps me feed the fire, and I teach him about draft and fuel. "It's important," I tell him, "to know how to start every fire with only one match."

"How come?"

"Because," I say. "One day you may find yourself having only one match."

We sleep very little as Kelli wakes for feeding and I tend the fire around the clock, checking it at two in the morning and at four, and restocking it at six for breakfast. Kelli has contracted mastitis. With Mason it was preeclampsia. With Madeline, it's mastitis. Fever comes on like death and she writhes on the couch. "Make it stop," she begs me. "Oh, God, make it stop." I sit on the floor by the couch and hold her hand and tell her I will make it stop, that it will stop soon. I curse the gods that torture her. "It burns," she says. "It burns." I feel her forehead. Her fever is soaring. I bank the fire and open a window until she shakes with chills. Then I shut the window and stoke the fire. Mason stands at the edge of this spectacle. "Dad," he says. "Is Mom okay?" I pull him close. He doesn't take his eyes off her as she arches her back in pain. Madeline cries from the bassinet. "She'll be fine," I say. "She'll be fine."

At five years of age, Mason was excited to be a big brother. But he was also nervous to hold his sister, nervous that he would do something wrong. I recall holding her out to him while he danced from one foot to another. "What if I drop her?"

"You won't drop her," I said.

"But what if I do?"

He gets his nervousness from me. When he is a father, I imagine, he will chase speeding cars down his street, waving his arms in the air, cursing their feckless ways.

But if he is nervous, he is also curious. He has asked many questions about his sister, about childbirth, about breast feeding. And I talked with him. I told him the story of his birth and Kelli's preeclampsia and bed rest. Each story prodded more questions. As with most five-year-olds, his world was made up of questions that became more complicated over time.

"Dad," he said one morning over breakfast. "Did the big buildings fall on my birthday?"

It was a subject that came up infrequently, but one that he had keyed in on whenever someone asked when his birthday was.

I paused, considered my response, and set my coffee cup down. "Yes, they did," I said, taking the less-is-more approach.

The question came almost as a non sequitur, catching me off guard. One day, I knew, we'd have to have the talk about how those buildings crashed to the earth. We'd have to talk about outward, unforeseen dangers.

Here's a related memory from that time. It is a Saturday morning not long after the New Year, Madeline just beyond a month old. I am in my office writing about my family and the hotel we run. I am thumbing through *Running in the Family*, as I do very often when I feel the story slipping away, when I feel the language going slack. It's a book I always keep near at hand. A kind of manual. Madeline is cooing on a blanket near the bookcase. Kelli is cooking breakfast. The thick scents of bacon, coffee, baked bread, and tamarack hang in the air. Outside, the skies are pool water blue and cold in the way that waters your eyes. From the living room, where Mason is playing with his action figures, the stove radiates waves of dry heat. I slip into the kitchen to refresh my coffee and talk with Kelli.

"Dad?" we hear Mason call from the living room.

I sip from my coffee and turn.

"Dad, something's wrong."

He is standing in front of the woodstove, pointing up. The white sting of fear strikes fast and electric. The black stovepipe that runs from the stovetop to the ceiling has popped its seam and come loose from the ceiling plate. The pipe leans slightly and spews foul black smoke and soot, and sparks shower the carpet and couches. I tell Kelli to get the baby out of the house. "Mason, get outside." He starts to cry. "We're fine, buddy," I say, softening the tone. "Just go outside."

The smoke detector begins chirruping steadily. After I shut down the damper, I put my leather gloves on, stand on a chair, and grab the stove pipe. But the gloves are too thin, the pipe too hot. In one fluid motion, I leap off the chair, dash to the kitchen, and return with four hot pads. Back on the chair, I try with no success to reconnect the pipe to the ceiling plate. Sparks are singeing my hair and the house is filling with black smoke, and even with the hot pads and gloves, the pipe is burning my hands. Desperate, I cock the stove pipe at an angle so that the upper sleeve binds against the lower shank, preventing it—I hope—from crashing down and begin pulling burning wood from the belly of the stove and dropping the chunks in threes into a scuttle. It takes three trips to convey the burning wood from the house. I dumped each load into a backyard snowdrift. Kelli and the kids stood in the front yard.

Half an hour later, the fire is dead, the smoke mostly cleared, and Kelli has brought the kids back inside. We're fine, if shaken. That night or maybe a few nights later, I have a nightmare that the house is burning to the ground and I can't get to my children. They aren't screaming, but I can hear Mason's searching voice, hauntingly calm. He just keeps saying, "Dad? Dad? Dad?" The dream rattles me so much that I get up, grab Mason from his bed, and pull him into ours. Madeline is fast asleep on Kelli's chest. I lie awake looking at all of them and thank the gods I have cursed and thanked for this—for this very moment right here in the long quiet of night.

Ondaatje, *Running in the Family* 165

Orwell, George. *1984*. New York: Signet Classics, 1981.

It topped a leaning stack of volumes, this book. And that stack stood next to my bed. It was summer 1993, the summer after my *second* disastrous freshman year. Dan, my pledge class brother, owned a house and rented several rooms out to guys in the fraternity, and that summer I moved my few belongings—my red trunk, the army duffle bag stuffed with clothes, a backpack, a guitar, several milk crates filled with books, and the Smith Corona motormouth—into the house. The tower of books was my personal challenge. While I had always been a reader, more or less, I was also a slow reader. Unlike my friend Spenser, who could plow through a fat book in a couple of hours, I spent days, weeks, and sometimes months in a single volume. My slowness was something of a badge of shame, as I interpreted it as a kind of brain defect, a kind of mental handicap. Also, my mind wandered from the page, and so reading, while hugely pleasurable and transporting, was also arduous and time consuming. Hence the need for a challenge.

I put fourteen books in a stack and promised myself that I would read each and every book cover to cover that summer if it killed me. The fourteen books were a mixed bag. Among the stack you could find Stephen King's *Skeleton Crew*, Kerouac's *On the Road*, Salinger's *Catcher in the Rye*, Edward Abbey's *Monkey Wrench Gang*, John Grisham's *The Pelican Brief*, Voltaire's *Candide*, and Orwell's *1984*. The thinking here was that I would increase my reading speed by forcing myself to shove through a stack of books. I would time myself with the first book, and then compare my time with the fourteenth book.

My friend Chad loaned me the copy of *1984*. He was a Cedar City local whose parents had ties to the university. Something of a wild man with a rat's nest of dark crazy hair, Chad donned, almost always, soccer shorts, a T-shirt, and sandals. In the winter, he wore jeans and lace-up boots. We spent our evenings driving around the brushy outskirts of town in his Ford Tempo (cool because he bolted a set of bull horns to the hood) listening to Ministry and smoking a bowl. Or we would clear the entire day and weird-out on acid in the red-rock mountains. We were both avid readers and aspiring writers. We were both loyal fans of Hunter S. Thompson and all things countercultural. We had penchant for the subversive. And so it followed that the more we smoked, the more paranoid we became. Not just paranoid that the white van two cars back was a narcotics sting operation lying in wait for the likes of us (especially me, a guy who had been busted in Arizona just a year earlier). Or that any one of our friends was secretly working for the police so that we might be ratted out as the dope fiends we were. But paranoid in the bigger, tin-foil hat, The-Man-is-Bringing-Us-Down kind of way. If the weed wasn't enough to inspire all kinds of wacko thoughts (and indeed it did), then Orwell's magnum opus certainly went a long way in painting the American landscape in ominous shades of gray hammer-down darkness.

As it happened, it was the first of the fourteen to read. And as it happened, Chad had it on extended (read: permanent) loan from his high school. Like Strasser's *Rock 'n' Roll Nights*, this volume is also stolen property. And like R'N'RN, I still have the copy. A stamp adorns the inside flyleaf with the following information:

PROPERTY OF
IRON COUNTY SCHOOL DISTRICT
CEDAR CITY HIGH SCHOOL
BOOK No: *14795*

Following the stamp, which I have X'd out in red ink, I have written the following snooty note also in red ink:

Aquired [*sic*] for a most noble purpose—more noble than its purpose on library shelves I assure you.

Honestly, I didn't think I would ever get through the book. Typical of Signet editions, the typeface in the book is microscopic and crowded, leaving only a thread of a margin on the page. An economic and not aesthetic decision on their part. Its pages do not invite marginalia. But as I thumb through it looking for keys to a past nearly lost to a perpetual cloud of pot smoke, I find markings here and there (all in red ballpoint), super insightful marginalia like "direct irony," and "yes!" But the markings are few. An underline here, a checkmark there. Nothing more. The book sucks you in. It's a sweaty-paged thriller. And I was thrilled. It was, I think, one of the first books I read that felt truly *deep* and *heavy* and *substantial.* For a hungry, cynical, and mostly stoned young man, this book was a volatile cocktail of high-octane ideas and cataclysmic realizations. I didn't see Orwell's book as a science-fiction warning. I saw it as a prophecy. The world contained within its pages wasn't Winston's world. It was *our* world.

Summer 1993 was a frenzy, politically. Bush senior, who was, in my viewpoint, dangerous, had just been replaced by this new guy Clinton guy. But the person who votes Democrat, as I had, in conservative southern Utah, is a lone voice in the howling wilderness of right-wing extremity. I recall one night, for instance, when I was at home in my room reading *1984* when a knock came to the door. It was Alton Lee, one of the founding fathers of our fraternity. He was older in a way that made him look forty when he was likely in his late twenties. I had scarcely exchanged more than a dozen words with him during my first year, and here he was at my door. Tall and muscular, Alton bore exaggerated features that made him look like some strapping dude plucked from a fable or cartoon. Dark hair, enormous chin, all brawn and brio. "Got a minute?" he asked,

I sat up and motioned for him to come in.

He asked all the generic stuff. How was my summer? How was work at the telemarketing place, blah, blah, blah. Then he looked at my book, and said, "You know that isn't too far from the truth."

I said I agreed and that it was scary stuff. And this is when he started in on his campaign. A campaign against this Clinton guy. "Right now," he said, "there are 400,000 Korean troops training across the Mexico border waiting to invade." He told me they were going to invade at any moment now that Clinton was in office, because they were in cahoots with one another, the Koreans and Clinton. A communist plot. But he had land, Alton did. And firearms. And horses. "I want my brothers safe," he said. "In one year from now, our country will be a communist nation, and we have to prepare." It would be our *Red Dawn*, he said, referencing the 1980s film about a Russian invasion of the U.S., and how a mountain-savvy group of kids would defeat the entire army. Talk about *deep* and *heavy*. Little did I know at the time that Alton was an ardent Birch Society loon—all God, guns, guts, and glory. Little did I know at the time that myriad strains of paranoia were afoot. The stoner's paranoia fades once the THC exits stage left, but this kind of paranoia was endemic. Encoded. But because Alton intimidated me, and because I was a junior active who had just bombed out of school, and one who was developing an unseemly reputation as a stoner in a throng of Mormonism, I didn't want to differ too much. I didn't want to get into that mind-numbing debate of my-team-is-better-than-your-team. And there wasn't a small part of me who just wanted to be accepted by everyone. As a consequence, I just said, "Wow" a lot and nodded my head and clucked my tongue, and, when appropriate, I would draw an example from *1984*.

And he would say, "Exactly."

But when Chad and I talked, it never occurred to us to grab a gun and dart off into the hills where we could skip out on paying our taxes. Our take was different. We would be the daredevil, stunt-pilot reporters at large, the sons of Dr. Thompson who would scrape the bottom of reality and display for all to see the dregs of hypocrisy and righteousness. So while Alton went from brother to brother, from room to room, preparing for Armageddon, Chad and I sat in front of his word processor and dreamed of how we would shake the world.

Enter *The Thunderground*. We would launch a newspaper for the upcoming fall quarter. An underground tirade. This would be our *Tattler*, our *Rambler*, our *Spectator*. We had dubbed ourselves Gonzo journalists. It was up to us to warn the public of the looming shadow of Republican hypocrisy, greed, and warmongering. We felt that Bush Sr. hadn't had his feet held to the fire sufficiently enough while he was in office, so we would step in. It was up to us to pick up where Orwell had left off in warning the masses of the wickedness of authority.

Our school mascot was the Thunderbird. The campus paper was titled *The Thunderbird* (later renamed *The University Journal*). And our answer to that administratively controlled rag was *The Thunderground*. We dreamed big. Our first issue was a single sheet of white printer paper with 12-point typed text. At first blush, it looked like the first page of a term paper. But we didn't see it that way. We saw it as razory, defiant, exclamatory, and dramatic. We printed maybe sixty copies and dropped thin sheaves around the student center where people picked up their weekly editions of *The Thunderbird*. And then we waited, our insides all a-roil over what was sure to be a massive backlash, or, what exactly? What would the reaction be? How did we expect people to react to a sheet of paper that looked like this:

THUNDERGROUND

"Those to whom no problems occur are asleep at the wheel of truth."

—*John A. Widstoe.*

Good morning America! How are you living today? Blind as yesterday? The answer: unfortunately, yes. Well—it's time to wake up and smell the bitter truth. Take a look around. You are about to drive off the road of life.

In <u>The Thunderground</u>, our purpose will not be to provide the 'right' answers to America's problems, but moreover, offer an alternative point of view. Some of the issues discussed in this paper, [sic] may break the integument of an unconsciously comfortable naivete [sic] that seems to blanket our culture as we know it. The following is a list of possible questions to be addressed in future editions of <u>The Thunderground</u>.

—Why is it hard to have confidence in the motto, "To serve and protect?"

—Why does the government refuse to acknowledge the ideal solution to the drug problem in America?

—How much power does the LDS Church have over Utah politics and are they striving to become an oligarchy?

"The first generation of reformers may be ignored, the second may be prosecuted, but the third will shake the world."—Unknown author.

That was it. That was our entry into the mad hatter world of alternative media. It would make us huge, we were sure. It would make us infamous, we were sure. It would likely make us wanted! Big Brother was no match for our sheet of paper and hard-hitting, in-yo-mutha-fuckin-face, muscular prose! We half-expected the police to teargas us. We half expected helicopters to bob over the campus green. We half expected the FBI to ramrod our doors. We half expected anarchy. And we secretly wanted it.

What we got instead was what you would expect: nothing. Maybe two people even read it. One girl using a courtesy phone flipped the sheet over and scribbled on it while nodding. "Uh-huh, uh-huh, uh-huh, uh-huh . . ."

That was it. And that was all. It didn't even amount to a blip, a ping, or a pixel on a vast field of light. A tiny weenie of a thing.

But we were undeterred. There was too much at stake. Our lives! Our freedoms! Our country! We were patriots! So over a bong of stinky weed, we plotted out the next issue.

Issue #2 looked similar to the first (i.e., term paperish) with one exception: we made a bigger header. We managed to coax Chad's doohickey of a word processor into enlarging the font as well as altering the font so that it was, to our thinking, wacky and edgy and eye-catching.

> Thunderground
> "Old man what the hell you gonna kill next. Old timer who gonna kill next?"—Roger Waters.
> THE INTERNATIONAL DRUG TRADE: THE MONEY TO BE MADE; TOTALITARIANISM, WHAT we unconsciously look for in our government to protect us from the truth.
> Well, what the fuck . . . let's talk about drugs. Let's talk about our government . . . . More to the point, let's talk about our government DOING drugs. Politicians getting laid, loaded, and lying about it.

The tirade ambled on from there, as if drunken and belligerent, and discussed not Clinton's alleged "uninhaled" pot smoking or his bouts with other women, but centered on George H. W. Bush and his ties with Noriega and drug trafficking. Issue #2 was a mess and poorly researched, and poorly written (more my fault than Chad's). But we felt like we were fighting the good fight, somehow.

At night, when I wasn't getting loaded or trying to get laid, I could be found in my small rented room reading *1984* or knocking out story ideas for the next issue. Alternately, Chad and I could be found on the outskirts of town with the stereo cranked with bloodshot eyes convinced we were living a Gonzo daydream, that fame and something called fortune were just around inevitable corners, and that we had been gifted voices that spoke for our entire restless generation. But it soon became clear that we had differing ideas and visions for *The Thunderground*. He wanted to take on the big political issues of the day. He wanted, for instance, to delve back into the Iran-Contra scandal to see if two rubes like us could unearth an unforeseen detail. His was a global picture whereas I wanted to take on homegrown issues like the university's administration, student fees, matters of church and state. And Chad did too, but he was tentative and perhaps rightly so. Both of his parents worked for the university in highly visible positions. His father was a professor and his mother was a high-end administrator. It would not bode well for them if it had been revealed that their son was disseminating foul-mouthed, incoherent diatribes around campus. It wasn't just the language or subject matter that would have been unseemly (though they would have added to the unseemliness), but our little rag aimed to rock the boat in a decidedly don't-rock-the-boat-if-you-know-what-is-good-for-you culture.

Looking back, it seems inevitable that Chad would fade away from *The Thunderground* and that I would carry the flag. The first two issues assumed the voice of "we" while issue #3—which took on local football players and their misbehavior (which I described as "Cro-Magnon") at school dances—switched to the first-person singular. Sample slammer: "MEMO TO THE STUDENTS OF SOUTHERN UTAH UNIVERSITY THAT GIVE A SHIT ABOUT THEIR AMERICAN RIGHTS, CLYDE PETERSON, BRENDA JOHNSON, AND SOME PERSON NAMED TESSA THAT NEEDS TO GET A NIGHT JOB.

The issue looked the same except that I had single spaced my rant and had added "An alternative newspaper" beneath the header.

If I had half-expected a response or backlash from the drivel *The Thunderground* had dispatched, I also had a sneaking hunch that it would just as easily be ignored. That is, until I decided to rail against the conservative majority who were, in the spring of 1993, calling for the ouster of the newly formed GLBT club. I typed up another single-spaced issue that was honorable in intention but bumbling and naïve in delivery. It was a hot-button issue and my pro-GLBT club stance was very much in the minority. Everyone, it seemed, was writing to the editor of the campus paper calling for the club's removal. Even a secondary alternative news leaflet thingy titled *The Mosquito*—which lasted one issue—debuted, responding to my paper in particular. Days later, our alternative papers were featured in the local paper, *The Daily Spectrum* (the daily that advertised for the sportswriter position I would apply for some five years down the road) under this headline: "Two underground newspapers debut at suu." While I was miffed that most of the coverage favored *The Mosquito* and made some swipes against *The Thunderground*—"two pieces of legal size paper stapled together, contain[ing] a quote from 12th President Zachary Taylor"—that was "badly written" (as one student aptly put it), I was punch-drunk and sky-high giddy that I had been *noticed*, that I was in the middle of a newspaper fight. (Later I would learn that the editor of *The Mosquito* called his best friend at the *Spectrum* and had asked him to run the story, hence the lopsided reporting; not that I am still bitter after all these years. I'm just saying.)

Meanwhile, students were writing into *The Thunderbird* in response to *my* paper. One student had even confused the two, prompting the editor of *The Thunderbird*—Don Scanlan, my English 101 instructor—to respond:

> EDITOR'S NOTE: It is the staff of *The Thunderground*, a publication in no way affiliated with *The Thunderbird*, that has printed the accusations against the football team mentioned in Mr. Anson's letter."

I was walking tall in those days. I was smoking a tobacco pipe and scribbling in notebooks, high on the printed word, and high on Orwell. Everything I wrote felt necessary, a wall of words to beat back the encroaching Big Brother I had read about. The more response I drew, the more serious I got about my mission. I came up with a penname, D. W. Hunt, as in Dog Will Hunt, taken first from the Primus song "Jerry was a Racecar Driver" and more loosely from the southern axiom "that dog don't hunt." But hunt I did. I was a mudhound, looking for any shitstorm to stir. I also changed up the format of *The Thunderground*. Subsequent issues featured columns so it looked more newsy. I printed it front and back on colored paper. I got a po box so people could write me directly, and they did. I started including a little image at the end of each issue, random shit I would put on the photocopier: a cigarette package with nubbed-out butts; a smattering of little American flags on toothpicks; a pair of forceps; a barcode, and so on.

Soon, I even had faculty members write me with carefully crafted phrases like "You may NOT quote me, but you can say that I support ————." Of course a good many people knew I was the one behind the mask of D. W. Hunt, and that thrilled me too. My phone would ring with tips. You should look into this, or that, they would say. I would spend late nights working on the issues (and therefore not on my homework) and would hit campus at 6:45 a.m. to unload stacks of my flyer. One morning after I had circulated my current issue, I stopped for a cup of coffee in the student center and watched in teeth-gritting anger as a high-level administrator gathered up my stacks and dropped them one by one in the trash. It was the clearest and most vivid sign that Orwellian powers were at large and that my paranoia wasn't paranoia at all. How else could I interpret such an act, such brazen censorship? But if there was anger in such considerations, there was also orgasmic joy. If what I was writing didn't matter, if what I had to say hadn't hit a nerve, if my writing was a vapid tract of irrelevance, then why trash them? And so there was a kind of sick pleasure I got out of watching that smug, suited man drop my late night's work into the garbage. I was winning, or so I thought.

For five years, I produced the *Thunderground*. For five years, I drew the ire of my enemies. Once, someone even produced an imposter version of my paper with the headline "Thunderground threatened!" "by B. S. Hunt." That part—the "B. S." business—was clever on their part. So was their choice in picking pink paper. It was what I would later call The Case of the Pink Imposter Paper Caper. It was a twisted form of flattery. Toward the end of my undergraduate daze, our small university had created an e-mail system onto which one student, who was deeply involved in student government (and who had started dating Mary, my ex-girlfriend), blasted out this mass e-mail:

> If you are a student or faculty or whatever; please take a moment to read this e-mail. Yesterday, yet another tirade entitled The Thunderground (Volume Three, No. 15) was available on campus . . . It IS Brandon Schrand's right to express his intelligently constructed and biased drivel; though he apparently does not have the spine to sign his name to it.

And so on . . . Truth is, I liked boasting two identities. I liked having an alter ego. D. W. Hunt was a lot of me and a lot of fiction, too. Parts of him I made up as if I were writing a novel. What would D. W. Hunt do in this situation? I would ask. He was his own man. He was braver than I could be. He was smarter than I was. He was cranky and fitful and passionate. He was the daydream version of myself. He was my second face, my Mr. Hyde. While Brandon Schrand penned his whimsical columns for *The University Journal* (formerly *The Thunderbird*), D. W. Hunt was rock, rock, rocking the boat. He was my license, my mask, my guard, my aide-de-camp on the battlefield of Orwellian wars.

In my last year of college, I made one final push to move *The Thunderground* into an actual magazine format. I converted my room in the Sigma Chi house into a makeshift production studio. I ordered newsprint graph paper and Exacto knives (old-school news production). I built a long production table with a built-in light box. I used the laminating machine at the telemarketing company to make "Press Passes" that read "THUNDERGROUND: We'll print damn near anything you want!" I came up with a business plan with advertising rates, print run, costs, the whole works. I drafted a slogan:

THUNDERGROUND

A STUDENT MAGAZINE

INDEPENDENT

.

PERIOD

I opened a checking account and loaned the magazine two hundred dollars (a small fortune to me then). Then I gathered a staff of the brightest writers and artists on campus and held a meeting. Everyone was on board. The meeting dragged on for nearly two hours. That was January 13, 1997. I still have the agenda and minutes. Eight people attended the meeting. That would be the one and only meeting of *The Thunderground*. I would not meet my not-yet wife until that spring at Lake Powell. Graduation became the goal, and I was preparing to move home for the summer. So I had a tough decision on my hands. Focus on the magazine. Or focus on finishing my classes. I chose the latter and let *The Thunderground* fade away.

Another form of flattery. A fraternity brother who was a year behind me in school revived *The Thunderground,* and with the help of one or two people published a handful of issues that made better use of technology and graphics. "We're honoring your legacy, Schrand," he had written in a letter to me. "This campus needs a second voice." Soon, though, they abandoned ship when graduation and grad school applications neared. Since then, there have been a few attempts by people I don't know to pick it up for a few months, when some issue twisted their titty, when some perceived threat of Orwellian heavy-handedness rapped at their door.

In the end, I lashed all the issues together in "Thunderground: A Waltz through Barbed Wire: The Chronicles: 1993–1997."

As it happened, I did, in fact, finish the leaning tower of books that summer. But it was Orwell's that made the biggest impact. His novel was a call to action, and I obliged.

Potter, David. *People of Plenty: Economic Abundance and the American Character.* Chicago: University of Chicago Press, 1958.

Had I not had the heavy-barreled pistol of graduate school aimed squarely at my head, I would never have picked this book up. Would never have given it a first glance. Would never have wandered into that dusty corner of the bookstore where books like this live. This was fall semester of my first official year of my master's degree at Utah State. I had enrolled in the required theories and Methods of American Studies seminar, and the list of texts was wholly intimidating, a veritable boot camp of intellectual grit. I was all in. We read Leo Marx, Henry Nash Smith, Patricia Nelson Limerick, Rupert Wilkinson, William Cronon, David Shi, Thoreau, a slablike anthology of pithy critical pieces on American Studies, an entire issue of *American Quarterly*, and, among others, David Potter's *People of Plenty.*

For the uninitiated, the cover of Potter's book—or at least my edition—features a black-and-white photo of an American skyscraper with an American flag flying at its corner. The photo was both iconic and dark. A picture of promise and doom. That the photo was shot close to the building, from the bottom up, with the photographer craning his lens skyward, adds to the ominous, inevitable story of a capitalistic society dwarfing its practitioners. A story beyond the human scale. The story of abundance. The skyscraper as God, as talisman, as Holy Scripture. As totem. The skyscraper as sanctum, sanctuary, cathedral. Put our money in the sky, in the clouds, the buildings seem to say. Closer to home, to our maker. Something about that photo on Potter's book grabbed me the more I read it.

This is how I read it. With pens, destroying each line with highlighting and underlines and marginalia, sticky notes interleaved like imperial flags of conquest and nation building. I read while walking, tripping over curbs, falling off stairs. I read on the toilet, before bed, the first thing in the morning. It was the only way to get through such a text: by way of maniacal engagement. Make the book your world. Put the blinders on. Eat fast food. Forego laundry. Don't comb your hair. Wear hats instead. It was a crazy time, an indulgent time. On Fridays during our marathon binge drinking at the local bar, the White Owl, we would argue theory back and forth, each of us dragging in this quote or that quote, our voices shrill and passionate. Ah! Those golden days when everything existed in abstract, ethereal terms. David Potter's book was intellectual exercise. His was no tract, no diatribe, no Thomas Paine manifesto, no call to action. It was a call for awareness, for dialogue across disciplines. It was, well, abstract. But then so was graduate school.

So was the world.

Our seminar met in the evening, once a week. The drill was your standard seminar stuff. Our professor would introduce a work, then we would read it over the course of the week, then reconvene to discuss the book the following session. And so it was with David Potter's book, the book that flashed its knowing black-and-white photo. That structure, the grainy waves of amber glass and steel, and the flying flag, our heart-joy! "For next time," our professor said. "Read Potter."

But there wouldn't be a next time. Not in any ordinary sense, anyway.

On the morning of Mason's first birthday, one week after we had been assigned to read *People of Plenty*, I was brushing my teeth in the hallway, where I could keep an eye on Mason, who was in his high chair in the dining room, and still talk to Kelli, who was in the bathroom. We had been discussing his birthday plans for later that day. Kelli was blow-drying her hair. Then someone on NPR said something about a plane or maybe two planes having hit the World Trade Center. "Can you turn that off?" I asked, motioning to her hair dryer.

"What?"

I pointed to the radio. Mason's birthday cake sat on the dining room table next to a book of mine for class. "Something's happened," I said.

Our professor had canceled class. "In light of today's events," the e-mail had said. "We'll pick up with *People of Plenty* next week."

Skyscrapers and books and flags. The things that were once abstract now irrevocably, undeniably concrete. Concrete in earth-crashing ways.

I was scheduled to teach at 11:00 that morning. English 101. Perhaps I should have canceled class. But I didn't. Canceling class, a university e-mail said, was "optional" in "light of the day's events." Please, it urged, be sensitive to those who will not be in attendance. Instead of canceling, I rode the bus to campus that day, and everyone on the bus was talking about that "day's events." People trying out their philosophies. Their theories. Who was responsible. Whom we should kill in retaliation. Who knew whom in NYC. And on and on. I said nothing. Like most of the nation, I was numb. Unable to process. I just kept wondering what in the hell I was going to say in class. Then I berated myself for not cancelling. How could we possibly discuss Rogerian styles of argumentation on such a day? How absurd! I couldn't bring myself to finish the final twenty or so pages in *People of Plenty*, much less give over any thought to a lesson plan.

In the end, I took only one thing to class. Instead of taking my textbook, my freshly graded stack of essays, my roll book, and dry-erase markers, I took a stack of white business-sized envelopes.

I said only two things. The first thing I said was that there were a lot of students at Utah State from the Middle East. I told them to put themselves in *their* shoes. Don't judge, in other words. They are our guests. The second thing I said was to get out a sheet of paper.

"Spend twenty minutes writing down anything you feel right now. On this very day. You can write about anger, sadness, confusion. Anything. Write it all down. And be honest. These are not for me. I won't be reading them. You will." At the end of twenty minutes, I asked them to fold their papers and seal them inside the envelopes. On the envelopes I instructed them to write DO NOT OPEN UNTIL SEPTEMBER 11, 2006. "It's a time capsule," I said. "I don't know what the future will be like, but you might be surprised by what you were thinking today five years from now. In five years, I suspect, I hope, we will know a whole lot more about this terrible event."

That was all. What else could you say? And with that, I dismissed them.

That afternoon, after Kelli got off work, we turned off NPR. We turned off the television. We turned off our phones. And we turned our attentions to Mason, our one-year old boy. The only innocent thing we knew or could recognize. He gurgled and jabbered and tore paper off his too-many presents. It was, embarrassingly, one of many birthdays when our money was flush and we bought everything in sight. That day, after class, as a way of reassuring myself that the world was still intact, I drove to a farming implement store and bought three die-cast toy tractors. *Every boy needs a tractor, if not three!* A green John Deere. A blue Ford. And a red Allis-Chalmers. Simple toys. Toys that spoke to simpler times, perhaps. Kelli also bought more toys on her lunch hour. And Mason tottered amidst towers of boxed presents, each brightly wrapped, ribboned, and stacked—a wild display of color and plenty. We snapped top-down pictures with an intensity and fear that daydreams were suddenly irrelevant, outmoded, a bygone fancy, a relic of yesteryear, or that the world might spin off its axis, or already had, and we needed to stop time and freeze this wonder. We needed reassuring. We needed to know that if we took pictures what was reflected back to us wasn't the crashing buildings on television, but was our small, beautiful, and fragile world. Our boy. Our suddenly tentative future. Our own heart-joy.

That next week, our professor turned to *People of Plenty* with a prefatory comment: "The world has changed, folks. The golden days are over. We have lost our innocence . . . Now," he said, clearing his throat and placing his hands on the table before him, "talk to me about Potter."

You could hear the air suck out of the room.

Proulx, Annie. *Close Range: Wyoming Stories.* New York: Scribner, 2003.

The stories closest to home are the easiest to overlook. The familiar always suffers in the face of the exotic or "other." The familiar is the residence of safety, of the here and now, of the otherwise banal. The exotic is home to the faraway, the far-flung, the daydreamy wonders of our imaginative worlds. Why, I wondered not so long ago, should I devote time to some Wyoming stories—stories inhabited by people I knew as well as I knew my own once-callused hands—when I could be reading Irving, Fitzgerald, Morrison? Why take up a book that aims to reveal the world into which you were thrown, a world whose mysteries you understand like a native tongue?

Everyone said Annie Proulx. You are writing about small town Idaho? Read Annie Proulx, they said, as if reading her words would unlock the stories I needed to tell. I had heard these urgings before, at Utah State, when I was trying to find my way back to my roots, arms out in a dark room, groping, and hoping to find familiar furnishings. Read Kittredge, they had said. Read Stegner, people had said. So I did. I read Kittredge. I read Stegner and a host of other western writers. And like the good student I had become, I ordered a copy of *Close Range.* When it arrived in my mailbox, I yanked it out of the bubble wrap—books in packaging, always gift-like!—I thumbed through its pages. Sized up the table of contents. Tested a few opening lines. Read the author bio. And then shelved it, satisfied that I could say, "Yeah, I have that book," fearful, too, that I may never get to read it.

I was in fact writing about small-town Idaho, a subject I had been sidling up to for years, and had even conjured in a few of my columns for *The University Journal* and *The Thunderground* back in college. The subject of so many of my bar stories. The old familiar stories. Always there in the background but seldom considered in any serious way, like insurance. Something you have. You got your stories. You know who you are. You're covered.

But in my second year of my MFA program, I did begin to consider my story, my upbringing in a serious way. That's when I began to take my own stories seriously.

That's when I started reading Annie Proulx's short stories. True, she was pulling her colors off the pallet of fiction, and I was working the canvas of nonfiction. And true, she is a genius and I'm a bonehead and our writing could *never* compare. But the landscape, urgency, and narrative fabric felt communal. Like the same deep well from which we hoisted our truths.

We were still living in the small logging town in those days. Days filled with the scent of split timber. The whine of the mill saw a dirge in our midst. Dreamy, constant, something you could put faith in. The summer before my third year was one I will not forget anytime soon. Because my TA stipend expired at the end of each year, our income was lopped off in the summers. Bills stacked up on the dining room table unopened. Why open what you can't pay? Why face that kind of debilitating data? Creditors called daily while I fought off aphids, ants, and partridges on our garden terrace. We were broke in all the known ways. Hand to mouth. Paycheck to paycheck. Debt dogged our dreams.

Then one afternoon that debt came knocking at our door. Mason, who was towheaded and four at the time, answered the door. "Daddy," he said. "It's a policeman." We had been put on notice. Pay up or else. Pay up or we'll see you in court. Pay up or go to jail.

Mired in debt, in an ocean of unforgiving numbers, numbers that demanded you render them to zero with money you didn't have, we sat there that afternoon holding the police-delivered notice. Kelli cried. Mason asked what was wrong. He was scared. The police. The tears. I was gut punched, miserable. To have your young son see that kind of thing. To have the police rap at your door. My god, I remember thinking (in a shallow, vulnerable moment), what will the neighbors think? It was as if we had returned to the days in Logan, to our rat-infested apartment behind the grocery store, which meant, to me, that we hadn't gotten anywhere. All the hand-raising and sacrificing had led nowhere. It was as if I had returned to my falling down ways, the ways in which police were always at the fray waiting for my one sure, inevitable misstep. It's not fair, I kept telling myself, the boy's voice too shrill in my own head. It's easy to feel sorry for yourself in those moments when the concreteness of math, of numbers, of amounts due remain unmovable, inert, and real in the face of your inability to do anything about it. It's easy to feel sorry for yourself as a police officer waits on your broken porch for your admission of guilt.

Finally, I had no choice but to call my grandmother and ask for help. We borrowed nearly two thousand dollars, assuring her—insisting, in fact—that we would pay her back. As soon as the student loan check arrived in the fall, I promised. Something about robbing Peter to pay Paul. An old routine I knew too well.

But it was a promise I kept.

During the days, while Kelli worked in a large office in the administration building on campus, I burned through the mornings by writing and reading. When I wasn't reading collections of essays, or when I wasn't plugging away on a lazy summer novel, I would leaf through *Close Range*. Mason would play with action figures on the living room floor—*Spongebob Squarepants* blaring in the background—until the neighbor boy would show up in his dirty white underwear and ask to play. After we ate a simple lunch, PB&J and grape juice, we would hit our usual routines of me pulling Mason in a wagon around town. We drew strange looks sometimes in that small logging town. I was out of place.

I was a young, capable man whiling away his afternoons with his son—surely, a mother's job—when I should be working.

But I *was* working. On my thesis. My book. And on a number of essays I kept shipping out the door. I needed my summers for writing. It was a conversation Kelli and I had many times. And to her undying credit, she goes down as one of the few people in the world who would tolerate such financial calamity in order to let her husband fidget at his computer, sweating out words, with the long, faraway hope that it might, just might pay off.

Chasing rainbows and pots of gold and the daydream of putting down words just so.

So it wasn't that I was lazy. Okay, a little lazy. A lot lazy, if I am honest. But I tended to work hard in ways that weren't visible or tallyable. It's an occupational hazard that doesn't square with my rural background. Among the many virtues of manual labor is that you—and others—can see what you have accomplished. You can see the stack of lumber. The framed wall. The moved irrigation lines. The bucked bales of hay. The holes dug, and posts sunk. The wire strung. And so on. Passersby can take note should they elect to do so. No fence there one day. The next day, a fence. It's the kind of life and work that the people who walk around in Proulx's stories do. Measurable work. Of course, writing doesn't work that way. At least not in the usual, measurable sense. If you are lucky enough to publish something, then you have some tangible thing to hold and say, "See? This is my work. See, I am not lazy."

But they are just words. They lack utility, weight, or substance. Words are like kites, pretty playthings you fly in the sky. That's what the sagebrush part of me says.

On the writing front, I had been struggling. I had undergone many, many months of rejections. Most of them form rejections. I started saving them, especially the ones when the editors took a moment to jot a note to me. Writing, it was becoming clear to me, was a lonely, dire occupation, made all the lonelier with each rejection. Each rejection a small failure that would add up, cumulatively, to big-picture, you're-fucking-your-family-over failure. Can there be anything more discouraging than to see bills pile up alongside an even larger stack of rejection letters?

But I was a bullheaded lug if nothing else, committed to punching words into a keyboard and hoping some kind of story would emerge, a story I might recognize. A story that would be at once familiar and other. A kite in the sky. Proulx's stories always charted out an elegant and revelatory otherness in the narrative tapestry of the familiar. I entered her stories knowing something of the landscape, the buck-brush, the lupine, rotting fenceposts, charcoal skies. The whiskey bars. The broken lovers fated to spend their lives in broken places. But then something would destabilize me and my senses. Something other. It was, I thought, something I wanted in my own stories. I needed to look back on my childhood in rural Idaho and chart out the otherness.

And so as the rejection letters arrived weekly, and as the bills mounted, and as I threw cans of pennies at the partridges in my garden, and as I pulled Mason around town in his wagon, and as the mill saw sang, and as Kelli worked in her large office, and as I sent off essay after essay, and as I thumbed through *Close Range*, I began to live on little more than faith in the alchemy of words. I began to learn firsthand what Hemingway was talking about in *A Movable Feast*: "I was always hungry with the walking and the cold and the working," he wrote. In the evenings, we drank bottom-shelf magnums of red wine. Screw-top stuff. Vinegary wine that came in jugs and boxes. And we would sit on our front porch, a wide-mouthed broken thing, and look out over the rooftops of town, and I would say, "If I could just get an essay accepted at a great journal!" or "If I could just get one chance!" And Kelli would say, "You will!" And I would bat my hand her way, brushing off her optimism, which I took to be dangerous. Best to err on the grim side. That was my view. My view, always the dour view. Her view, always the hopeful view. Faith in the familiar and a hopeful view guided us through those tentative summer months with the heat and the empty cupboards and the dashed dreams and the work yet to be done.

Proulx, *Close Range* 187

Stegner, Wallace. *The Big Rock Candy Mountain*. New York: Penguin, 1991.

Wallace Stegner stepped out from the shadows on a fall afternoon when I was neck deep in books and ideas at Utah State University. I was seated in a basement-room seminar of the English department and the sun was crashing west outside, filling the smallish windows with wild firelight. Two books on the syllabus felt hefty and daunting: *Angle of Repose* and *Beyond the Hundredth Meridian*. When I held each in my hand, two voices emerged from my mind, two competing personalities, a duality that had caused so much tension all my life. One voice said "Yes! Big books! I will read these big books and become smart and bookish!" And the other voice, a residual echo left over from my fuck-up undergraduate days said, "Hell, no. There is no *way* I will actually wade through all of these pages." "I mean, sure," the voice reasoned, "I will read half or more, but not all."

Then you learn a thing or two about Wallace Stegner. You learn, for instance, that he grew up on the move, in the midst of wagon tramps, bootleggers, and rainbow chasers. That he grew up in the prairie wind that he could, at a moment's notice, blow in any direction for hundreds of miles only to land in rough, untrod territory. That all his life he suffered from an insatiable hunger for roots and books that could and would tell him who he was. That he felt divided between his eastern bookish daydreams and his western boyish ways. That he himself could speak volumes to that thin line between the worlds of the here and now and those of the printed page. You learn, for instance, that he too grew up among the Mormon faithful and had befriended them. You learn, for instance, that both of you had known with fierce intimacy certain places around the West. Places like Little Cottonwood Canyon. Fish Lake. Mink Creek. Sardine Canyon. Bear Lake. And on and on. Here is the utter shock of recognition. If you ever needed permission to write truly of the places that moved you most, Stegner was the man to issue such permission. If you ever needed to know that your appetites for all things eastern and your loyalties to all things western weren't a matter of your own isolated madness, then you needed to look no further than Stegner. You needed to look no further than *Angle of Repose*. Or *Beyond the Hundredth Meridian*. Or any other book in his expansive body of work.

The more I learned about Stegner, the more I fevered. Connections—or so I saw them at the time—abounded. He had earned his undergraduate degree in Utah as I had. And one of his early research interests involved an obscure nineteenth-century figure, Clarence Dutton. Mine involved an equally obscure figure, John Codman. Stegner borrowed—or so I argued, and perhaps rightly so—his title for *Mormon Country* from Codman's own 1874 volume, *The Mormon Country* (Stegner even quoted old Codman in his book).

While many of my peers trudged through Stegner, I soared beyond the final pages and took on his other books in addition to my regular reading load. I read *The Big Rock Candy Mountain* (from which I would borrow my thesis title, "A Country to Lift the Blood"); I read *Wolf Willow* and, of course, *Mormon Country*. And many others. Here, finally, was a life worth emulating. *What do you want to be when you grow up?* Had anyone asked me that in those roaring days, I would have said—and with no sense of shame—Wallace Stegner. He was a fiction writer, essayist, biographer, conservationist, teacher, all of it. What else could you want?

Interleaved into my copy of *The Big Rock Candy Mountain* are three yellow legal sheets stapled together and filled with notes.

At the top of page one, I find "Thesis Notes" and the date 5.6.02. Mason wasn't even two years old. Kelli was working at her temp agency, running away (from me) on weekends to see her family. And when I wasn't in the bar, all aswim in booze, I was swimming in Stegner's words, trying to find my way to some kind of plausible thesis. I was becoming frantic, and the more frantic I became, the more I drank and the more I read.

And all I read was Stegner. It was a full-throttled Stegner Bender, and I was itching for a fix. But my very attraction to his work and his example also became a source of inner turmoil. I couldn't focus. On the one hand I had this Codman character I had plucked from the past. The old salt I had first read about when I was boy. I felt a real and dire need to legitimize his ghost, which would, I thought, legitimize me. So Codman was my thesis topic. Absolutely. Lock it in. Get to work. Graduate. Codman will lead you to the promised land of an advanced degree!

But I am a Libra. And even though I don't believe in such nonsense, I have often been hamstrung by decisions. This or that? Stay or go? Chicken or beef? Red or white? East or West? So the scales of the Libra suit me. Always weighing. Always hemming and hawing. Would Codman be my thesis topic, or would a personal story emerge? And how and when would I know? When would I, like, *know*-know?

When I read *The Big Rock Candy Mountain* (whose central family's name is the Masons, which is similar to my son's name, whom we named before I read TBRCM: Mason Fitzgerald), I was struck by the electric impulse to write my *own* family's story, and that would be my thesis. But when I read *Beyond the Hundredth Meridian* or, later, *Mormon Country*, I just knew I had to write about Codman. Days would pile up. I would gather sources, prowl the Internet. E-mail librarians around the globe for clues. And then on a random Sunday morning, I would snatch *Angle of Repose* off my bookshelf. AOR's verdict only made matters worse: write a family story based on Codman's life, as Stegner had with Mary Hallock Foote.

So rich was my confusion, my split interests, my inability to choose, that my own thesis chair couldn't remember from one day to the next what my thesis was about. Nor could my peers. At the bar, I would talk on and on about Codman. And then someone would say, "Wow, man. You've got a great thesis."

I would wave my hand at them and shake my head. "Dude, Codman's not my thesis." Blank stares all around. "I told you. I am writing about my family."

Two weeks later. Same bar. Same scene. And me: talking about my family settling the West. "I want to read your thesis when you're done," someone would say.

Then it was my turn to give a blank stare: "Dude, I told you I was writing about Codman. *Jesus* . . . Doesn't anyone listen to me?"

In the end, I landed on a topic as surely and squarely as if it were destiny. In the end, I settled on my family. In the end, tragedy sealed the deal. My biological grandfather died suddenly and I inherited a box of photographs, letters, and papers. Amazing photographs of my family (on my mother's side) settling Jackson Hole, Wyoming, at the turn of the century. Snapshots from another world, a storied world, so easily romanticized and Hollywoodified. Draught horses pulling timber from the woods. Settlers' work. Dirty-faced children in ragged clothes stand in the cheatgrass with the Tetons scraping the sky behind them, something straight out of *Shane*. A little girl squatting in the dooryard in her white dress and white shoes holding, of all things, her pet badger. Letters dated 1893, the year of Fredrick Jackson Turner's famous Frontier Thesis, the year of the Columbian Exposition in Chicago, the year of the great Panic, the year my great-great grandparents got married in Elwood, Nebraska: letters that talk of poverty, of taking in extra laundry to make ends meet, letters of births, of burying a child in the prairie sod. Story after story. This was no fiction, no daydream. This was the story of the West, at once ordinary and extraordinary, familiar and exotic. It was my thesis, my great Stegnarian chance. My *Big Rock Candy Mountain*. How, I asked, would the story of one ordinary family's westward migration square with the western master narrative I had learned about—and then, as grad students are charged to do—deconstructed? Would it differ? If so, how and where? Or would their story as interpreted through photographs, letters, and oral histories (then written down) merely corroborate that larger narrative? Ultimately, I was arguing for the ordinary, that the familial/familiar narratives added to, not detracted from, the surprisingly lively academic discourse on the American West. Mostly, though, I was just doing what I had been doing all my life. I was emulating the particular traits of yet another literary lion. I was making like a copycat and loving it. I wanted to be Wallace Stegner just like I wanted to be Kittredge or Marquez or Morrison or Hemingway or Irving. I wanted his life. I wanted to write what he wrote. Little surprise that I would stand in the shadow of his permissive example for so long. After all, he was the consummate Victorian. What is it with us barnyarders and our insatiable hunger for the high, marbled towers of a life we secretly see as stolen from us? Why do we suffer from the indefatigable "switched-at-birth" syndrome? Will we ever be comfortable in our own skin? And when I say "we" I really mean "I." I can't and won't speak for Stegner, or Wally, as his friends knew him, but something tells me that if we'd had the chance we could have compared cards and found some similarities in our hands. I suspect the same is true for so many young, restless West-sick young men.

And yet the differences! Talent and genius aside, the differences between the dean of Western letters and this wannabe student are something I failed to consider thoroughly in my days of shadowing his legacy. He wasn't a drinker, really. As Phillip Fradkin points out in his laudable biography of Wally, Stegner cut his drinking back to nearly zip once he started pining for cocktail hour. Nor was he a philanderer, so far as we know. The man wasn't a perfect husband or father (who the hell is?), but by and large, he was a stand-up guy whose only perceivable weakness, if we are to call it that, was the ability to hold a grudge over long periods of time. Why didn't I try to emulate those traits? The stand-up sober traits? The discipline and self-control? The traits of an otherwise congenial guy with a decidedly Victorian moral bent?

But I didn't pay attention to any of that. The way of the eager-beaver graduate student is to be engaged in a hyper-caffeinated way, to be always one step ahead of your officemates, to be the rising star, to win the sweeping praise of all the right professors. And so I set to the task of writing my thesis, "'A Country to Lift the Blood': Portrait of Westering Family Finding Home in the Tetons." Following Stegner's example, I lifted my title from another text, and in this case, that text was TBRCM. Bruce Mason, the protagonist in the novel (er, memoir dressed up as a novel) is on his way West, to his home, after having abandoned it for his eastern daydreams of the Ivy League and life in letters. "It was a grand country," Stegner writes, "a country to lift the blood, and [Bruce] was going home across its wind-kissed miles with the sun on him and the cornfields streaming under the first summer heat . . . But going home where? he said. Where do I belong in this? . . . Where do I belong in this country? Where is home?"

If all your life your dreams lie in the East but your blood courses through the West, what then? Can you point to one and say *home*? Can you put your feet down in a place made of dreams, of fiction? Can you hang your hat on the idea of a better life? Or is that better life the one you've got in front of you, the one you are pissing away at the bars, the one you let go to her parents' house every weekend? Truth? You have no idea where home is or how to get there. And because you are the eager-beaver graduate student you have convinced yourself that if you trace your family's lineage, indeed, if you lift and sift the blood, if you follow in Stegner's footsteps, then you might finally recognize the man-child who stares back from the mirror.

Something else I recognized. The beauty of a girl I worked with. I had only worked at the environmental consulting gig about a week when Erin—who had been on vacation—walked through the door. That she was beautiful was without contest. Petite, blonde, tan, and well put together. But she was more than eye candy. She was as smart as she was charming. As for me, I was the father of a toddler son, and husband to a wife who took off on the weekends. I wasn't the lean, single frat guy I had been in college. I was the fat married guy. When, exactly, does this happen? How cruel time can be. The fat married guy who harbors a secret crush on a stunning coworker is not the core of American tragedy, but it's a second cousin. It is the core of American sadness, perhaps.

Of course Erin scarcely noticed me. At first. But then a funny thing happened. Days turned into weeks, and then into months, and then into a year, and during the course of that time we grew close. Probably too close. She burned me CDs of her favorite bands and I suggested books she should read. When her birthday rolled around, I bought her books—*Out of Africa* and *The Unbearable Lightness of Being* and *Angle of Repose*. We flirted openly. Or I saw it as flirting. I thought it was going somewhere. But I didn't see it from her perspective. I was her "safe" guy friend.

But we got closer still. We would sometimes meet for beers after work or on weekends. At work we talked nonstop. And we laughed. We clicked in all the right ways. On the weekends when Kelli was gone, I would get liquored up and call Erin under the guise of some work-related thing, and then we would talk on and on. Once I stopped by her apartment and she gave me a tour and then a beer. We drank the cold beers in the hot apartment on her couch. She would cross her legs, and I would kick the bottom of her foot so her legs would uncross and she would laugh and kick me back, or fake-punch me in the arm. From her couch, I could see her bedroom and the bed inside and how badly I wanted to make love to her in that bed. It was a crushing want.

My gaze burned on her bed as I thumbed the neck of my beer bottle.

The closer Erin and I got, the more our coworkers started to raise their eyebrows. By all outward appearances, it would have looked like we were having an affair, which we were not. Our closeness was not, in any way, appropriate, however, and I think we both knew it. I certainly did. We crossed many boundaries. We passed notes at work like teenagers. I would rub her shoulders and find any excuse for physical contact which was, after a year, electric (at least for me). She would muss my hair, pinch my arm, or swat my leg. I would sit on her lap. Steal her pens. Shoot her with rubber bands. She would give me recipes and books and notes and more CDs. "I burned these for you last night," she would say, and I would go liquid. Once, at a company party at our boss's cabin, Erin asked me to teach her to play the guitar. Everyone was tipsy, including Kelli, who was also there. Mason was playing with a ball in the grass, and I was sitting next to Erin showing her a G-chord. She grabbed my hand with one hand and put it on her fingers on the fret-board. "Help me," she said, laughing.

"I will if you stop being a jackass!"

More laughing. So I would position her fingers where they needed to be. My fingers touching hers. My fingers moving hers. Fingers on fingers. Fingers moving fingers. Something about that. Something about that had Kelli staring right through us, stony faced.

So I couldn't have been surprised when Kelli wanted to talk a few days later. "What's going on between you and Erin?"

I played dumb. "What do you mean?"

"I see how you are together. What is going on?"

"Nothing," I said. "Honest to God."

"Have you slept with her?"

"No. No way." It was the truth. We hadn't so much as kissed, ever. And I told Kelli as much. "Swear to God," I said.

"She's beautiful, so I can see why—"

"Yes. You know what? She *is* beautiful. She is gorgeous. And we get each other. And we talk a lot and we're close. And she is probably one of my best friends, but we haven't *done* anything."

Unlike so many men who have faced this kind of firing squad, I had truth on my side. Nothing had happened. But if I am honest, I would have slept with Erin in a second had she given me the chance. I was a foolish, self-involved young man with a hard-on for any good-looking girl who passed by. But with Erin, it was more complicated.

"If you just had sex with someone," Kelli said carefully, "I could understand that. You're in the moment. It's physical. Whatever. But if you fell in love with someone else, well, that would be harder to take."

We were in our living room, on the couch. Mason was taking a nap. No noise but our breathing and the ticking of the clock on the wall. I hung my head. I gave her some half-hearted assurances that I wasn't in love with Erin. The saving grace of it all is that Erin, I knew, wasn't—and nor would she ever be—in love with me. As difficult as that was for me to swallow, it was also liberating.

The last time I saw Erin is when she invited me to her house for dinner. Kelli and Mason had already moved to Idaho, and I was set to leave the next morning on my great adventure. Erin prepared one of my favorite dishes: grilled lamb chops, asparagus, and couscous with a bottle of red. We had all night and the entire house together. That evening I will remember as wonderful and sad. We ate and talked and told stories and jokes and played the "remember when" game. We drank two bottles of wine and danced in the living room. That's when she told me she had a boyfriend. Twice during the course of the evening, she cried and I held her. We said nothing for a long while. Why she cried, is not for me to know, and it doesn't matter anyway. Before I left, we exchanged cards, handwritten, earnest cards. Hers contained a quote from Thoreau, and mine urged her to read Stegner. In the end, however, I gave her a hug, kissed her on her forehead, and took my leave.

It was the right kind of ending to the wrong kind of friendship. If it was the right kind of ending, it also signaled a beginning. The very next morning, I piled into my Land Cruiser and throttled north to see my family in our new home in Idaho. Tabula Rasa. The past as epilogue. Logan and my falling-down ways all one hazy memory, a smudge. Like it never happened.

Thompson, Hunter S. *Fear and Loathing in Las Vegas*. New York: Vintage, 1989.

But before that. Before I was married with my first child. Before all of that, there were still the vagaries of my truant young adulthood, the delusion and plenty of self-loathing to slog through. And one book that propped me up in those days of misbehavior was *Fear and Loathing in Las Vegas*.

In truth I first heard of this book in high school when I was extolling the greater literary merits of Jim Morrison, but there was a delay in finding my way to its story. When a friend reintroduced me to this book, I grabbed it and held on with both hands. Thompson's voice was irreverent and raucous and—not unlike Morrison's—very often incomprehensible. While my peers attended to the letters in Jane Austen's *Lady Susan* or to the bumbling innocence of Silas Lapham or to the dark side of Gatsby's lavish parties, I attended to HST, the Doctor himself. I once wrote a research paper for my expository writing class on Thompson's Gonzo journalism and even tried drawing connections between Thompson and the Roman satirist Juvenal. The paper was cobbled together from scant sources and wandered here and there, devoid of point or insight. In the end, its thesis statement was something like "Hunter S. Thompson is the Greatest Writer in the History of the World and All Mankind." But my professor was lenient and I managed a B. The paper, as I recall, had a crisis of clarity, brought on, no doubt, by the Chivas Regal I was drinking and the pot I was smoking while composing it. Added up, these accoutrements of the savage lifestyle of Hunter S. Thompson didn't do much for my research paper, but they did convince this fool that wisdom or something like it could be found in the sad and vacant dust-bin of abandon.

At some point not long after turning in my paper I decided that I would invite Hunter Thompson to give a lecture as part of our ongoing university convocation series. To make the pitch look official, I pilfered some university letterhead and envelopes from the student government offices and got to work. "Dear Hunter S. Thompson," I wrote,

> As the student representative on this year's convocation se-
> ries [lie], I am delighted to invite you to give a lecture on
> our campus this academic year. I have been a fan of your
> work for some time and would be pleased if you would ac-
> cept our offer. To be absolutely frank, though, I must tell
> you that your presence is not only requested, but it is re-
> quired. Our convocation series has been nothing short of a
> goddamn three-ring circus of jack-asses and salivating buf-
> foons [lie]. You know the people of whom I speak, surely . . .

I mailed the letter general delivery to Woody Creek, Colorado and waited not-so-patiently for a response—(in the letter I add-ed some iffy lines about how he should respond to my *personal* address, and not the *university* address). Within a week I received a response. But it wasn't from Dr. Thompson. It was from the vice president for student services, the man whose office meted out all discipline at the school. He wanted to chat.

In hindsight—which occurred the second I received the VP's letter—I recognized two tactical errors in judgment on my part. First, I failed to consider postal logistics. If the letter bounced back as undeliverable, which it did, it would go not to me, but to the university. Second, I signed *my name* to the letter. This was something I debated, and the decision to endorse the missive was not one I made easily. I was vaguely aware of an outside risk of getting caught, but I was so confident that Thompson would get the letter that I wanted my name attached to it in hopes that it would spark a correspondence between us. After all, I had reasoned, he had once written to William Faulkner. Thompson, of all people, would understand and appreciate my position.

The day I walked into the administration building to speak with the vice president is one I will not soon forget. I was on my second round of academic probation, which made my position all the more precarious. His office had a third-story view of the main parking lot and south side of campus. It was dark and austere and intimidating. When I stepped into the conference room my eyes fixed on the letter in the center of the enormous table. The VP—a veritable doppelganger of John Ashcroft—sat halfway down the table, and an elegant woman with silver hair sat at the far end, fuming. Her long, bullet-like nails clicked on the table. I recognized her as Lana Johnson, the chair of the convocation committee. My stomach slipped.

"I presume by now you know the nature of this meeting?" the VP started.

I nodded at took a seat at the end of the conference room, opposite Ms. Johnson. The first half of the meeting, which couldn't have exceeded five minutes, consisted of me "explaining myself," which I failed to do in any convincing manner. I felt woozy and faint and miserable. And when the VP produced my transcript and made casual mention of my poor academic performance (a move that strikes me now as remotely illegal), I quailed. The last half of the meeting vacillated between the VP and Ms. Johnson giving me the business—shaking fingers, stern language—and me apologizing, floundering in the trough of regret. "I have no excuse," I would say. "This was uncalled for," I would say. And "I have learned a great deal from all of this."

The next day I received the following letter again from the VP. "Dear Brandon," it read:

> This letter is to verify our discussion yesterday regarding your unauthorized representation of the University and the subsequent embarrassment which it caused the institution.

You were officially reprimanded and warned that any such future behavior on your part would result in disciplinary action being taken by my office . . . As we indicated to you, if you wish to make suggestions to the Convocation Committee for future speakers you would be welcome to do so.

Here in print lay the consequences for attempting to pull back the muslin that floats between reality and the fiction it inspires.

(Oh, but Irony!—the great doctrine of reality and fiction. Consider the power of irony. Consider my shock, when, fifteen years later, I received an e-mail asking me to deliver a convocation at this very school. The guy who failed convocation (see transcript on page 70). And the guy who was "officially reprimanded" for his "unauthorized" attempt at trying to lure the Gonzo man himself to campus for said convocation series is now invited back to talk about, what exactly? How *not* to be a fuck-up? How it is best to get straight As? How one should probably avoid jail, if possible? How to behave and not misbehave? How to act like a man, and not a lunatic boy? Aren't these all givens? Isn't that conversation, that convocation, over before it begins? Oh, irony, it abounds).

Toole, John Kennedy. *A Confederacy of Dunces*. New York: Grove Press, 1980.

As usual, it was my well-read friend Levi who suggested I read this book, and because I trusted his taste and advice (especially after he more or less commanded me to read Hornby's *High Fidelity*), I marched to the bookstore on payday and bought a copy. It was fall 1997 and the leaves on the trees were just beginning to yellow. I had healed from my nasty breakup with Mary and was starting to enjoy the single life again. I was going out again, to the bars, and had hooked up with a couple of girls. Nothing serious. I wasn't really looking for anything serious. Just a good lay now and again.

And that is when I started to spend time with Hannah, a beautiful short-haired brunette from Las Vegas. We were both English majors and had classes together and I teased her, mocked her (in the flirty, I'm-totally-into-you kind of way), and she dished back. It was a great vibe. But it was also problematic because Hannah was married. So, yeah, not ideal. But her husband was some loser named Dwight, a high-school dropout who smoked a lot of weed, sold bags on the side, and worked construction. Tattooed, with blonde, spiky hair, Dwight was one of those cake-eaters who called his inferiors "buddy," using it as a diminutive. It's what he called me the half-dozen or so times I had the misfortune of running into him, which was usually at a party. "Hey, buddy!" he'd say, and I'd flash a gritted-teeth smile while entertaining thoughts of punching him in the throat. Of course, Hannah was generally at the same parties, which made for some awkward moments here and there.

Soon our status as classmates escalated to study partners. And study we did. At the library. At night. For several weeks, it became a very regular thing, and then one night, as we walked toward my Land Cruiser, she stopped and faced me. "Uh," she began. And then: "Never mind."

"What?"

"I have to go."

A beat.

"O—kay,"

"I mean before I kiss you." She let out a half-chuckle, and turned and started walking.

"Whoa, whoa, whoa! Hey!" I called. It was dark and the fall air was chilly, and the sidewalks and parking lot near the library were lit by an orange halogen glow. She was walking away in a quick clip. "You can't just say that shit and walk off!"

She turned around and rehooked her backpack on her shoulder. "If I stay, I will do something I will regret, and I don't want to regret anything. So . . . goodnight." She smiled weakly and waved and walked toward her car.

Later that night, I was drinking with Spenser like usual. I told him about what Hannah had said, to get his read.

"Dude," he said. "You need to slam her like a screen door."

"She's fucking married."

"To a fuck-wad. You've seen the guy. He's a turd-burglar. He takes little boys on camping trips. I mean the guy didn't even finish high school. What the fuck is Hannah even doing with him in the first place? You tell me that?"

I shrugged and drained my glass. "I think it's trouble."

"If you fuck her?"

"Yeah."

"Why?"

"Because it will make me an adulterer."

"It will make *her* an adulterer, dude, not you. So, no worries."

"Yeah. No worries."

As soon as you say, "No worries," the worries begin to rain down, and this was no exception to that most inevitable rule. The worries begin when you give in to weakness, when you listen to the boy inside and not the man. The worries begin when you cross lines, break rules, vows. The worries begin when you find yourself alone with a married woman in your room in your fraternity house with an open bottle of wine. The worries begin there, when she unzips your pants and pulls you out. But you're all boy and boys don't think when someone has just sprung them from their trousers. Boys just do, and they typically do whomever is there. One minute, you're trying to do the stand-up thing. You're trying to be rational, wise, level-headed. But how quickly all that flies out the window in the course of a hand-job. And quicker still because the hand-job is connected to the blow-job, and the blow-job is connected to the sex-job.

But the second it's over, the second the popping-lights fade from your eyes, and your heart rate calms and you roll over and you both lie there heaving and naked and sweating, the second all that has subsided, then the worries become real.

Then, when there is a definitive lull, when the realization settles in like a steely dawn, she turns and looks at you, and you can feel it coming. It's so scripted, so predictable. She will say, *This was a mistake.* She will say, *We should not do this anymore.* She will say, *I am married and this cannot happen.* She will say, *I am sorry. We shouldn't have.* Part of you will be crushed, and part of you will be relieved.

But that is not what she says. Instead, she says, "We need to be careful."

Before Hannah leaves, she dresses, and says, "I need something." Her eyes scan my room. "Like a reason I came over here."

I look at her.

"In case someone sees me leave your house." It was a real

concern. We lived in a small college town and when a married woman is seen leaving a fraternity house, it could only mean one thing.

"Right." I think for a second and then roll over and grab *A Confederacy of Dunces*, which I had recently finished. "Take this." I hand it to her. Then, as if giving instructions, I say, "You needed to borrow it. For a paper."

She flips through it. "Right. For a paper," she repeats distractedly.

A cover story. A collaborative fiction. Lay down the fiction to mask the truth. One story on top of another. Like lovers.

"Is it any good?" Hannah asks.

"Yeah. It's wacky. Levi suggested it." Hannah and Levi moved in some of the same circles I did, so they knew one another well.

She laughs. "Well, if Levi suggested it, it will definitely be Levi humor. Know what I mean?"

Oh yes, I did.

For the next three weeks, we met in secret and humped like porn stars. Crazy, grabby, monkey sex. And for the next three weeks, Hannah carted *A Confederacy of Dunces* around. And eventually, she finished reading it. "It's hilarious," she said one day after class.

"I know. Levi has good taste. The guy's dialed in."

"I'll say."

At the end of the three weeks, I made a mistake. Or maybe it wasn't a mistake. Or maybe it was both a mistake and not a mistake. I told a girl whom I'd had a thing for that I had slept with Hannah—thinking, like the idiot I was, that my conquest would impress this girl and that my admission would ultimately lead to sex with *her*. But that didn't happen. What happened was that this girl then told Hannah's older brother, Clint, who also lived in Cedar City, who in turn told Dwight. And the gig was up. Hannah made one final visit, dropped off *A Confederacy of Dunces*, and said, "We're getting a divorce." She had been crying, and she started to cry again. "What were you *thinking*?"

I hung my head. "I don't know what to say. I'm sorry."

We sat there on my bed for a good long while, and then to break the silence, I said, "I suppose he's going to kick my ass now, Dwight."

A faint smile. She shook her head. "No, no. He didn't want to be married any more than I did. Christ, he's had his own affairs." She looked straight ahead, exhaled a deep breath as if she had been holding it all her life, and said, "I have to do laundry."

She started for my bedroom door and stopped. "It was a good story, by the way."

I knew she meant the book but I couldn't help but seeing it another way. The next time I saw Hannah (outside of class, where we had grown distant), was in the grocery store. At night. I rounded a corner of an aisle and there she was.

"Hey."

"Hey."

Each of us was trying to act casual to quell the avalanche of awkwardness and dread that had just crashed in Aisle 6 next to the Beanee-Weenies. I tried to make some joke or other, but to no effect. It was wooden like our whole exchange.

"So."

"So."

"So, you probably heard that I'm seeing Levi," she said.

I had heard this, and to be honest, I was happy for them. "That's great."

"We just click, you know?"

"I can see that."

"And—he's got great taste in books."

"Totally."

"Like you," she said, and looked at her shoes.

"Right," I said and fake-coughed. "Listen: you take care." And I meant it.

Eventually I would meet Kelli and we would marry and move on. Eventually Levi and Hannah graduated and moved to Chicago where they entered graduate school: Levi in finance and Hannah in library science. As time passed, Levi and I stayed in touch by phone and e-mail, and the spring before Kelli and Mason moved to Idaho, Levi called with good news. "We're getting married."

I hooted in the phone. "Congratulations, man! Seriously. You guys are great together." Which, of course, was true.

But I couldn't have been prepared for what came next.

"Hannah and I want you to be the best man."

I was floored. Of course Levi knew that Hannah and I had been together, so that conversation could not have been easy for them. But their request said a whole lot about them. It said they were great people. Hannah was a great woman. And Levi was a great man. He was a man I wanted one day to be like.

The wedding would be held in Flagstaff (where Hannah's father lived), but it was taking place on the same weekend as a Stegner conference I had been invited to in Cambridge, Massachusetts. It was what you would call a conundrum. Here, in one invitation, was the entrance into the daydream I had entertained my entire life. I would be on a panel discussing one of my favorite authors—a man who suffered from some of the same East/West anxieties I did—in a place I had only heard about in books. Words like Cambridge and Harvard and Boston conjured in my mind the sounds of bells ringing across great open lawns and the image of a genteel world where one could lose himself in the pursuit of grace.

On the other hand, I was asked to be the best man at a wedding of a close friend and his bride-to-be with whom I had an illicit affair that directly caused her divorce, but, in turn, brought her and Levi to the marbled altar of matrimony. It was a strange and winding plot with no small dash of irony, a plot that seemed more befitting of a novel or stage play than reality. And at the center of the plot there existed this one book, and as fine and rompingly funny as *A Confederacy of Dunces* is, I cannot look at it without thinking of Hannah and Levi.

Toole, *A Confederacy of Dunces* 207

In the end, I did the stand-up thing. I did what, I think, Stegner would have done: I took a rain-check on the conference, on Cambridge, on that beacon shining in the East, and committed to the wedding in the West.

It was a long drive to Flagstaff, so Kelli and I dropped Mason off with her parents and turned the excursion into a mini-vacation, one final venture before we made our new move to Idaho. In the car, I practiced my speech over and over again. I memorized each line and the particular kinds of emphases I wanted to place on each word. I had flubbed wedding speeches before because I had drunk too much Jack Daniel's, and I was not, under any circumstances, going to flub this one.

Nor did I.

Wallace, David Foster. *A Supposedly Fun Thing I'll Never Do Again*. New York: Little, Brown, 1997.
———. *Consider the Lobster*. New York: Little, Brown, 2006.

An apparition. There's no other way to explain how *A Supposedly Fun Thing I'll Never Do Again* and its author came rushing into my life. One day the book is not there, and the next day it is. Outside my office door at the University of Idaho. I found it in a cardboard box where I had asked my students to turn in their essays. On the afternoon I collected the essays, I spotted this book mixed in with the papers. No note. No explanation. It was just there. I glanced up and down the hallway, but it was empty. End of the spring term. Everyone was bailing for the summer.

Over one year would pass before I learned how that book arrived, without explanation, in my drop box. (Turns out a student of mine—one of my best and brightest—had dropped it in there. "I just thought of you when I read it. Keep it," he said. And so I did.)

Two or three days after I found Wallace's book, I walked across a stage before a large crowd of people and received what would be my second advanced degree. This was May 2006. I had completed my three-year MFA program and was officially no longer a student. Outside the day was clear and bright and smelled like summer, like cut grass, like linens on a clothesline, like a dream. And I stood on the lawn beneath the sky and maples, my infant daughter, Maddie, in one arm, and Mason to my side. Kelli snapped picture after picture. Maddie in her dress. Mason in a white button-down shirt, bow tie, and shorts. Me in my gown and sash and cap.

What firm ground. What freedom. What safety.

After pictures, I let Mason wear my cap. Parents and graduates alike point and smile at him, at us. And we laugh and stroll through the campus green.

Snatches from my journal then: "I can't believe I have graduated and am no longer a grad student. I couldn't be happier." And: "I've been offered some prize classes to teach next year" And: "Very happy."

Oh, the shore of safety, it comes.

A week or so after I walked across that great stage that signaled the end of so much and the beginning of so much more, I get online and buy train tickets. I'm taking my family to Glacier National Park for a much-needed vacation. At the train station in Spokane, the four of us cram into the only two available train seats on our car. It's 1:00 in the morning, and we're exhausted. Maddie is zonked out in her car seat on the floor beneath Kelli's feet, and Mason stretches out across our laps. My backpack, which contains David Foster Wallace's *A Supposedly Fun Thing I'll Never Do Again*, is stowed beneath my feet.

Outside it is ink dark save the flicker of town lights that rush by. I nod off now and again and wake to try to guess where we are. Then I force myself to stay awake through Sandpoint, Idaho, because that part of the train trip is terrifying and its terrifyingness is made all the more so at night, in total darkness. You know you have reached Sandpoint because the train slows as it crosses a mile-long bridge over the enormous (by western standards) Lake Pend Oreille (pronounced "pond-o-ray"). Anyone who has read Marilynne Robinson's *Housekeeping* will know straight away my fears about that part of the trip. The book opens with a horrific scene of a train breaking track on a bridge over a mountain lake in Fingerbone, Idaho—the fictional name for the real town, Sandpoint, Robinson's hometown. Speaking of her grandfather's job on the railroad as "watchman, or perhaps signal man," the narrator—Ruth—recalls his demise.

> He held this post for two years, when, as he was returning from some business in Spokane, his mortal and professional careers ended in a spectacular derailment. The disaster took place midway through a moonless night. The train which was black and sleek and elegant . . . had pulled more than halfway across the bridge when the engine nosed over toward the lake and then the rest of the train slid after it into the water like a weasel sliding off a rock.

With that scene burning bright in my imagination, I peer out the window and watch with dry-throat fascination the darkly haunting water that is betrayed by occasional lights flashing like phantoms on its surface. And while the train hisses and rattles across the bridge, and while my wife and children breathe and dream, I sit straight-backed and imagine the horror. The horror of knowing that if we broke track as the train in the novel had, there would be nothing I could do to save them. It's foolish to be hijacked by such thoughts, to run the scenarios, but I do. Even if we survived immediate impact, there would be no way out. And even if we got out of the car now sinking into the deathly murk, I couldn't pull my wife, son, *and* infant daughter out by myself. Okay, I think, Kelli could swim with Maddie. I would pull Mason out. But even then the water would be cold enough to kill us, especially Maddie. I wonder: will her car seat float like its own lifeboat or drag her down? If she's strapped in, do we unstrap her? If we keep her in the car seat, and if we have to exit through a broken window, say, will the car seat fit? You look at the size of the window, then at your daughter and size up her seat, and think: no. Best to ditch the car seat. You consider your surroundings. You can hear the groan of metal twisting, the screams of the other passengers. You can feel the icy water rushing in, a hell-black flood sweeping people to their doom. You see it all. The green dark. The flickering electrical system. The dying blue light. Bodies falling through the car as if down the dark throat of an elevator shaft. Straight. Fucking. Down. How much time would we have? Seconds. Nothing more. You would have to think fast. You can't let indecision ambush you here. Your lives depend on quick thinking. Still, though. Barring all of that, we would have to swim to the trestle and hold on. But what if we were injured on impact? Head trauma, a broken arm or leg? What about a massive gash caused by broken window glass? What if both parents are knocked unconscious? What if we were among the falling bodies, the soon dead? What would Mason do? Where is he? What would be his chances? Where is the baby? You feel yourself get sick in the stomach. Okay, okay, calm down. Don't go there. So: say we *aren't* injured, and say we *can* exit the sinking train, which is sinking all the faster with each crashing passenger-car dragging the whole beast down to center-of-the-earth depths, what are your chances of making it then? I think it through and think it through. I am not a good swimmer and would be lucky just trying to save myself, let alone my son. Adrenaline would help, but for how long? How to get him to the trestle? How good of a swimmer is Kelli? How will we make it? What if you are swimming up through the dark, and another car rolls down, falling right on top of you splitting your head open like a picnic melon? Would you see it in time to swim out of the way? No—no you wouldn't. Each possible scenario leads to a dead end, and each dead end is the result of you dragging them along on this journey in the first place. Finally, the question that arises out of this nightmarish cauldron of fear, the one that has been staring you right in the face for so long, is this:

Are You Man Enough to Save Your Family?
Well, Are You?

But the train doesn't jump track. It caterpillars across the bridge spanning the great dark lake, and soon we're in the woods. The fear dissipates, and I sit back and drift off, patting Mason's back. *It's okay. Everything is okay.*

At dawn, we slowly stir from our dreams and eye the passing scenery out the windows. Dense forest. An early morning mist. And a moose browsing trackside. "Look!" Mason says, scrambling for a better view. Several passengers snap photos of the long-legged, huge-racked bull. I take in the entire moment and think, *A guy could do worse than wake to this.*

After Kelli feeds Maddie, who will be six months old in a few days, we train-sway-swagger to the dining car for breakfast. Because I have done this route before, when I rode the rails to Boston and back, I recognize immediately where we are. Suddenly we're out of the trees in the high country. All willows and rivers and rock, a great open swath of wild country. "You know where we are?" I ask Mason.

He shakes his head.

"We're crossing the Continental Divide!"

First his eyes widen, and then he says, "Whoa," and then his face slackens into thought: "What's that?"

So I tell him. I say, "This is where rivers change directions."

He looks confused and so I set my coffee cup down and explain it to him.

He's impressed.

So am I.

On the observation car, Kelli reads from her book while Maddie sleeps, then, when Maddie wakes, Kelli reads to her. I read to Mason this book or that, and after a while, Kelli and I switch books or kids or both. And when I have time to myself, I read DFW as the *Empire Builder* rattles over mountain passes, from Spokane to Montana, eastbound into the West.

Because we are poor, we can afford to stay only one night in the main lodge, the large, timbered hotel seen on so many postcards. We spend the rest of our vacation in a little camper cabin down the road. It is small and charming and humble and just right. Something that looks as if it had been hammered together in the 1950s. It has a small kitchenette with a hot plate, microwave, and sink. A toaster. Coffee-pot. Fridge. The living room is also the bedroom, and there is a small wooden table and two chairs. A few small windows dressed in gingham curtains.

On our first day there, Kelli makes a list, master-planner that she is. "We need to buy some groceries. It will be cheaper that way." Meaning cheaper than eating out every night. "Agreed," I say, and we take a long walk to the main store in East Glacier and buy all the necessary stuff. Loaf of bread. Block of cheese. Cans of tomato soup. Top Ramen. Sodas. Juice. Coffee. A bottle of wine. And some crackers and candy.

Because it has been raining and snowing for the last few days, we hang out in the camper-cabin and play card games. We tell stories. Kelli reads her book. I read DFW. Mason plays with his toys. We're living our life. It's simple and we're poor, and we feast on grilled cheese sandwiches and tomato soup in a tiny cabin in one of the most beautiful places on earth. I am not sure what happiness looks like, but it might look like this.

The train home ended in chaos. We arrived in Spokane around 2:00 a.m. only to discover that we had left an interior light on in the Land Cruiser, and that the battery was dead beyond dead. And to be clear, the train station in Spokane is in a dodgy part of town and as a consequence, attracts a dodgy cast of characters, especially in the small hours. Put another way, it's not really a place you want to be hanging around with your wife, five-year-old son, and six-month old daughter.

Unlike airports that will send a truck out to jump-start your vehicle, this train station does nothing. When I asked for help, the beefy man behind the counter looked irritated.

"I've got a family," I said. "And a baby."

He glanced over my shoulder where Kelli, Maddie, and Mason stood waiting. "You might try a cab driver."

So a cab driver it was. For ten dollars. But I didn't care. I just wanted to get my family home.

Home. Our Victorian house in the small logging town came into view at sunrise, just before 5:00 a.m. "Finally," Kelli said as we pulled into the driveway. Yes, finally. Sort of. We were home but learn quickly, after the pocket-pat-down and the whole "Do you-have-the-keys?/I-thought-you-had-them routine, that we were locked out of the house (our house key was on the spare set inside). Of course we were locked out of the house. Of course. The whole train experience became my own *Supposedly Fun Thing I'll Never Do Again* kind of experience (Wallace's was a cruise ship.)

The upshot was that the bathroom window was unlocked, so drawing on my old panty-raid skills, I crawled through the window and hit the floor (which hurt much worse this time around).

That trip home. It's one of our favorite stories to tell. It's a keeper, that story.

I could tell, then, when I first opened that copy of DFW's ASFTINDA—the book that fell from a cloudless sky—that here was a writer who knew how to work and how to obsess (in all the good ways). Who else could write a one-hundred-page hyper-footnoted essay about a cruise? Only someone driven to turn over every last detail, to wade through the minutia, to examine and then reexamine, and continue to ask why, why, why?—that's who. Only someone who takes seriously what it means to be both human and curious and to better one's life by engaging in the world. By asking the questions. Why is ——— so ———, and to what end? What does it mean, ultimately, or what could it mean? And what does ——— say about me or us? What can we learn about *x* by examining *y*? Consider the variables, the nuance, the lobster, the everyday, the sacred ,a the profane. I could tell at first glance (which led to an immediate and deep immersion into his book) that I was in the presence of a mind of special intensity, a mind unwilling to let a topic go because everyone else in the Total Noise of the world always let it go, never, in fact, thought to engage in ——— topic, and this fear (of the human's insatiable appetite for catastrophic indifference) is what fueled the engine that drove the intensity in the first place.

For many years we had been crossing to safety, or trying to, and the distant shore was finally discernible in the midst of uncer-

tainty. I was waking up in a new country made up not of consequences but of new opportunities and new books, and DFW's
was the clearest. Resist the Total Noise, he said. Because that's
the true way to live. Cut straight through it. It's the only way to
be a better human, to be a better society. Swim upstream. Don't
settle for the lowest common denominators of Old Navy and
American Idol and Applebees and this Big Box and that Big Box
and the Jonas Brothers and the *Twilight* books featured on the
Kindle. That's all noise. Taken as a cumulative force, the Total
Noise is just as much or more destructive than my old falling
down ways. Everything is representation. The on-demand world
is a world of simulacra and euphemism. Authenticity is an anti-
quarian notion. Hyperreality is the new reality. It's a 100% More
Real Free World, Baby, and DFW saw the writing on the wall.
Sure, he taught me about writing and engaging a subject matter with an obsessive, relentless eye, but he also taught me what's
at stake if you turn your back on the noise. He taught me what
hangs in the balance, and what hangs in the balance is the future, which means my children.

You could do worse than entering his mind. And the door-
ways are his books, but once you get in, there is no getting out,
and that is its own kind of reward, its own kind of geography of
authenticity.

Wolff, Tobias. *This Boy's Life: A Memoir.* New York: Harper Perennial, 1989.

This might be the beating heart in the great master narrative of East vs. West, of gentility vs. tyranny, of man vs. boy. It was natural that I found my way to this book, or that it found its way to me. I read it the same summer I read DFW, sometime after Glacier. I read it in my hammock on our patio on lazy afternoons. I read it in my tent when camping, and I read it in the park while Mason darted in and out of the play structure and Maddie tottered around the sandbox. It's a classic, a top-fiver, a go-to book.

But beyond Wolff's native genius is the story itself, of how his mother took her son west to try to make a go of it. Go west, young man. Go West. Dream of the East. I understood at some visceral level the many layers of the story, of what it means to fall down on your way up, to be both a young man and a boy. It's the cruelest of things. Or can be.

The following spring, in April 2007, when I was fresh into my new job, my new office, this new life, I decided to teach Wolff's memoir in my nonfiction class. It's a good pick because it's a good book, to throw a simple description on it, but it's a good pick because it appeals to what you might call a kind of Idaho demographic (of course, its appeal is much, much wider than that). The students recognize things. Like place names. Concrete, Washington, for instance. Or Salt Lake City. They recognize, as I had, the story about what it means to feel like you are trapped and sentenced to death in rural America, and that you will die young. Or that you will live, destined to tramp the muddy streets of some western shantytown until you grow old and die, and they plant you with all the rest at the scrubby edge of town next to the highway and its fast-food wrappers and broken bottle glass. Trapped because leaving = betrayal. Trapped because man = boy. Trapped because your life = a script. You know how it is to end, and so do your neighbors. And not a few of these students can also recognize the kind of home-front tumult that stomps around in its pages.

I remember well the days when we were wrapping up our discussion of *This Boy's Life*. "Why," I asked the class, "is Wolff singing at the end? After everything he has just gone through, why is he singing?"

There was a beat. Then, slowly, a hand went up. It was one of my brightest and best writers, a kid named Mark who always—*always*—wore a Yankees sweatshirt. "Because if he's not singing, then he's crying."

Exactly.

It was during those days of rereading and teaching Wolff's boyhood memoir that I got some news about my own. It works like this. One day you're counting the rejection slips, the passing of days, weeks, months, and then you get an e-mail with the title of your book in the subject line. Your heart knocks around and your stomach flip-flops and your hands start shaking as you open the message (which takes like six years) and it reads, "We need to talk. Call me asap."

My book, as it turned out, had won a small literary contest and would be published.

Well, holy shit.

Sometimes things do work out, though. Sometimes the boy becomes a man, a husband, a father. Sometimes you find your way into telling your own story, and sometimes it's your own story that will save you in the end.

That night, after we had received the news, Kelli and I called our friends and met downtown for dinner and we celebrated by spending fortunes we didn't have. On our way home, it was dark and the moonlight fell through the maple trees on the street and on the sidewalk. Because Kelli had walked downtown from her office to meet up, I had ridden my bike from home and was pushing it back. We walked at a slow and meandering pace, laughing. My god, we just laughed at the whole thing: at us, and the luck, the pure luck of it all! Giddy, I threw a leg over my bike for a quick celebratory ride. I tried to pedal forward but got tripped up and crashed to the sidewalk. Kelli looked back and I lay there under my bike, moonblind, laughing.

Kelli is in stitches. "What did you do?"

Through belts of tears-down-your-face laughter, I manage, "I crashed!"

She calls me a dumbass and we laugh more.

You laugh hysterically because if you don't, you'll cry. You'll cry at the beauty of chance, of survival, at the arrangement of the stars. You'll cry because you made it down the long passage in one piece. You'll cry because you wrote your way out of the shantytown story. You'll cry because you wrote your way out of your younger self. You'll cry because Look at Your Family, Man! You'll cry right there on the sidewalk beneath the moon, that white scrape on the black field of forever. You'll cry beneath the maples. You'll cry when your wife reaches down and pulls you up from your spill. But you don't cry. Instead, you laugh. My god, how you laugh!

Nothing could be better.

Nothing could be better than your own crashing heart-joy flying in the face of the odds against you—the odds which the boy in you conspired to create. The odds which the man in you conspired to tear down, brick by terrifying brick.

Oh, the odds, they are out there. And you can either listen to them and how they call you down, and how they will tell you that boys born into sagebrush country will get stuck in the ruts of their own design. That boys born into sagebrush country stay forever boys, out there somewhere, at the edge of town gunning their junkers into their most certain fate. That boys will be boys will be boys will be boys, and their stories will beget stories—the same stories—on through the generations. Those are the odds. And it's the madness, the duplicitous nature of the man-boy, that aids and abets the odds against you.

It's you against you, man.

So you choose not to listen to the odds if for no other reason than the sheer predictability of that story. It's an old story. Stone-old. Ancient. Third verse, same as the first. And all the rest.

The misbehaving boy in me has always wanted to live in a novel, to walk around in a plot culled from some preexistence of the incandescent imagination. He has always wanted to attend one of Gatsby's parties, to have visited Dinesen's African farm or have accompanied Aureliano Buendia when he and his father discovered ice. If he is honest, he will admit wanting to be Marquez, Hemingway, or Stegner if for just a day. The boy is indentured to story if nothing else, and he struggles to find where the ragged edge of the page ends and the undulating world picks up. But the man knows what is actual, what is right there before him. The man knows well the heartsick fear of the sinking doom in the coal-black water, and how—as best as anyone can—to avoid it.

But listen: buildings go up in smoke. Cars speed through neighborhoods. Planes fall from the sky. Trains jump track. You can't chase away all the dangerous things with flailing arms and curses. This much I know. The dangers I can chase away, however, the ones that stare back from the mirror, the ones that seem wired into the genetic map, the master narrative, those I can, and have, chased away, more or less. I still fall down, just differently. I erupt over small things. I am impatient with my children on mornings when we're running late. I am preoccupied with work, with tasks that dog me. My attentions are divided. Sometimes I have too much wine. On the very rare occasion, I wake with a headache (the operative word there is "rare.") In these regards, I am not that much different from other fathers. The pressures and fears and worries and impulses are always there, for most of us, I would guess. And like so many fathers, I am always trying to slow down and stop the clock. I am trying to pay attention.

But when I am not paying attention, I have my family to call me on it. Not long ago, I was lying in bed reading when Madeline—who was not yet three—crawled up on my chest, grabbed my face with both hands, and said, "Look at me, boy!"

Look at me, boy.

Well, okay then.

It's a story we bore the hell out of our friends with, but for us it is a great story.

Here's another story, one that might even save your life. It's an ordinary story, one devoid of police lights, the clang of the jail-cell door, the yawp of the boy gone mad in a world of books. Because it is an ordinary story, it lacks plot, dramatic tension, or arc, but in my view it's a top-fiver, a go-to story. Sometimes I see the scene from above: the wide open green of a university soccer field in northern Idaho. The sky is one sheet of blue July. The day is still, dreamlike, save for a breeze out of the west. At the edge of the green, you see a woman jogging, a cyclist. But in the middle of the green you see a young man and his two children: an eight-year-old boy and a three-year-old girl. Two small kites float against the field of blue. Each child tugs at a string. The young man darts back and forth between them, ensuring that the strings don't cross. *Careful*, he says. *Careful.* It's astonishing, he thinks, how the day feels windless, but up there the kites climb and wave, steady and strong. It's the girl's first time flying her own kite, and it requires both of her hands. The boy lies in the grass and flies his kite effortlessly, like an afterthought, a daydream. And the young man could die right there, imagines, even, that on the day he slips out of this life, it will be this moment, this scene shot from above that he takes with him into the blue beyond. This good story. This boyish heart-joy. The young man knows that no one will ever write a better story than this one. Because it is true, and because it is his own.

Your Usual Acknowledgments

I have in many ways a charmed life. I have reached the shore of safety (or some semblance of it) after so many years, and I have but one person to thank for staying when she could have gone; for supporting me when others would've given up hope. That person is my wife and life partner, Kelli. She's a cape-wearing, kick-ass, walk-on-water, super-heroine mother and spouse. I also have to thank my amazing kids, Mason and Madeline, who rock my world every blessed minute.

Legion are the peeps who deserve a shout out, who offered advice and who kept the faith along the way. First, my colleagues at the University of Idaho: Mary Clearman Blew, Kim Barnes, Jeff Jones, Ron McFarland, Daniel Orozco, Joy Passanante, Alexandra Teague, and Robert Wrigley. I couldn't imagine a better or more talented community of writers to work with than these folks. Second, my students (present and former) who teach me, as the old cliché goes (and yet it's true!) every bit as much or more than I could ever teach them. I thank each and every one of them, but some deserve a special nod: Matt Bauman, Sonya Dunning, McKenzie Gibbs, Eric Hayes, Jennifer Houston, Bethany Leach, Julie Lilienkamp, Mark Lindquist, Bethany Maile, Mary Morgan, Kiri Oler, Andrew Parks, Aaron Poor, Chelsia Rice, Deb Ricks, Jamaica Ritcher, Kendall Sand, Molly Schultz, Ann Stebner, Cara Stoddard, Tyler Stoddard, T. J. Tranchell, Robin Tucker, Anna Vodicka, Matt Vollendorf, Paul Warmbier, and Matt Zambito.

Third, for their care and time and engagement in this book, I thank the following: Kristen Elias Rowley (a champion to the end); Dinty W. Moore (who is awesome in All-Things-Nonfiction); and Sonya Huber (for her wicked intelligence and kick-ass advice on the manuscript). Also to Stephen

Barnett who provided excellent advice in the latter stages of the book. But mostly my agent, Matt McGowan, who was there from the beginning of this book and never once flinched in his faith.

I'd like to give endless thanks to the Corporation of Yaddo for giving me the time and space to work.

Portions of this book have been published elsewhere, and I thank the editors for their enthusiasm: Ben George, editor of *The Book of Dads*; Evelyn Somers, of *The Missouri Review*, and Mary Morgan at *Fugue*.

Source Acknowledgments

"Brinley, Bertrand R. *The Mad Scientists' Club*. New York: Scholastic, 1965"; "Flaubert, Gustave. *Madame Bovary: Life in a Country Town*. Vol. 2 of *Norton Anthology of World* Masterpieces, 6th ed., edited by Maynard Mack, Bernard M. W. Knox, John C. McGalliard, P. M. Pasinetti, Howard E. Hugo, Patricia Meyer Spacks, Rene Wellek, Kenneth Douglas, and Sarah Lawall. New York: Norton, 1992"; "Hemingway, Ernest. *The Old Man and the Sea*. New York: Macmillan, 1980" and Hemingway, Ernest. *The Sun Also Rises*. New York: Macmillan, 1987"; "Hinton, S. E. *The Outsiders*. New York: Laurel Leaf, 1968."; and "Morrison, Jim. *Wilderness: The Lost Writings of Jim Morrison*. Vol. 1. New York: Vintage, 1988" first appeared in a slightly different form as "Works Cited" in "Pick Your Poison," *The Missouri Review* 31, no. 3 (2008): 29–42.

Portions of "Irving, John. *A Prayer for Owen Meany*. New York: Ballantine, 1989. ———. *The World According to Garp*. New York: Ballantine, 1989"; "Kittredge, William. *Hole in the Sky*. New York: Vintage, 1992"; "Ondaatje, Michael. *Running in the Family*. New York: Vintage, 1982"; and "Potter, David. *People of Plenty. Economic Abundance and the American Character*. Chicago: University of Chicago Press, 1958" first appeared in a slightly different form as "Comparative History" in *The Book of Dads: Essays on the Joys, Perils, and Humiliations of Fatherhood*, edited by Ben George (Harper Perennial, 2009), 139–55.

Portions of "Menand, Louis. *The Metaphysical Club: The Story of Ideas in America*. New York: Farrar, Straus, and Giroux, 2002" first appeared in a slightly different form in "Why I Stay," *Fugue: 20th Anniversary Issue* 38 (Spring/Winter 2010): 184–94.

*My Ruby Slippers: Finding Place
on the Road Back to Kansas*
by Tracy Seeley

The Fortune Teller's Kiss
by Brenda Serotte

Gang of One: Memoirs of a Red Guard
by Fan Shen

Just Breathe Normally
by Peggy Shumaker

Scraping By in the Big Eighties
by Natalia Rachel Singer

In the Shadow of Memory
by Floyd Skloot

*Secret Frequencies: A New York
Education*
by John Skoyles

Phantom Limb
by Janet Sternburg

*Yellowstone Autumn: A Season of
Discovery in a Wondrous Land*
by W. D. Wetherell

To order or obtain more
information on these or other
University of Nebraska Press titles,
visit www.nebraskapress.unl.edu.